ENGAGING *and* RETAINING
EMPLOYEE TALENT

A FAST ACTION DEVELOPMENT GUIDE | Includes 7 Action Plans to Impact Talent Results

Center for **TALENT RETENTION**

www.keeppeople.com

Center for Talent Retention
600 17th Street
Suite 2800 South
Denver, CO 80202

Copyright © 2001-2005 by Center for Talent Retention

All rights reserved. This book, or parts therefore, may not be reproduced in any form without permission.

Library of Congress Cataloging-in-Publication Data

Barton, Derrick R.
    Engaging and Retaining Employee Talent: A FAST Action Development Guide/
    Derrick R. Barton, Kimberly E. Egan
    p. cm.
    ISBN 0-9714204-0-8
    1. Employee Retention   2. Engaging Employees   3. Employee Turnover
    I. Barton, Derrick R.   II. Egan, Kimberly E.   III. Title

Printed in the United States of America

Center for TALENT RETENTION

www.keeppeople.com

Table of Contents

Acknowledgements — 2
Preface — 3

How to Use — 4
The Manager Role — 6
Manager Actions and Qualities — 8
Building Skills and Capabilities — 9

Coaching Performance — 19
    24 — Coaching Performance Solutions
    41 — Coaching Performance Worksheets

Supporting Work — 55
    57 — Supporting Work Solutions
    77 — Supporting Work Worksheets

Providing Feedback — 89
    91 — Providing Feedback Solutions
    110 — Providing Feedback Worksheets

Establishing Credibility — 123
    125 — Establishing Credibility Solutions
    144 — Establishing Credibility Worksheets

Show Caring — 157
    159 — Show Caring Solutions
    177 — Show Caring Worksheets

Communication — 191
    193 — Communication Solutions
    211 — Communication Worksheets

Personal Actions — 225
    227 — Personal Actions Solutions
    245 — Personal Actions Worksheets

Acknowledgements

We would like to thank the managers we have worked with for sharing their personal stories and experiences. These stories and experiences were the inspiration for the actions we <u>all</u> must take to engage and retain employee talent.

We would also like to thank our families—Gene, Betty, Sherrie, Makenzie, Chase, Bill, Chris, and Kevin for helping us understand what's most important.

Derrick R. Barton & Kimberly E. Egan

Preface

Critical Talent Results

For any organization to achieve its business goals and long-term success, the organization must achieve the following employee talent results:

- **ENGAGE** the talent you have to perform at your highest levels
- **RETAIN** the talent you need to support your business strategy
- **ATTRACT** the talent required to prosper long-term

Fast Action Development Guide

The Fast Action Development Guide is a comprehensive resource containing over 100 solutions designed for managers to TAKE ACTION to impact the seven manager capabilities needed to engage and retain employee talent.

This Guide provides numerous solutions managers can implement in the next 48 hours, 7 days, 30 days, and 90 days to positively impact the critical manager capabilities, and make a real impact on their talent results.

About Us

The Center for Talent Retention is dedicated to building an organization's capabilities to deliver human capital results. We are the leading expert on "taking action" to increase employee engagement and reduce turnover.

We offer an integrated system of talent solutions guaranteed to equip your organization, managers, HR professionals, and work groups to make a real impact on talent results.

If your organization demands results…you need to work with the Center for Talent Retention.

How to Use

Simple, Fast, Targeted Steps are the Key

The Fast Action Development Guide provides over 100 solutions to help managers communicate with employees, support their work, coach performance, care about them as individuals, establish credibility, provide feedback, and impact talent through their personal actions.

Managers impact engaging and retaining employee talent through seven manager capabilities. These capabilities are further defined into distinct manager actions describing what you would see a manager do on-the-job to impact talent results.

Coaching Performance	Supporting Work	Providing Feedback	Establishing Credibility	Show Caring	Communication	Personal Actions
Provide direction and coaching to help employees perform	Offer the resources and support employees need to be successful	Deliver frequent and specific feedback to help employees improve their performance	Role model words and actions that build credibility with others	Take action to show your employees you care about them as individuals	Create an environment to encourage comfortable two-way dialogue and the exchanging of ideas	Manage the way you handle difficult and frustrating situations

Each solution includes simple, easy-to-follow steps, as well as supporting worksheets and templates to help to you take action with speed, there is no need to get bogged down in the planning—review the solutions, select the ones that fit your situation, and take action!

Implementation Steps

Step 1: Review your Results

Before you take action, you must determine which manager capability will make the greatest impact on engaging and retaining your employees.

- **Review your self-assessment or feedback data**

  Review your data and identify your strengths, average capabilities and current weaknesses.

- **Identify what's "most critical"**

  Identify what's "most critical" to engage and retain your employees.

- **Where do you have energy?**

  Most importantly, identify the area you really want to improve and determine if taking action would be worth your time and energy.

How to Use

Implementation Steps continued

Step 2: Focus your improvement efforts
Select one area to work on first. There will always be time to come back and do more. It's better to do a few things very well, than a lot of stuff "halfway".

Step 3: Create a Plan
Review the action plan you selected, and determine which solutions you will implement.

Note:
- Don't dilute your efforts by selecting too many solutions to implement.
- You may want to make modifications to a solution to tailor it to meet your unique needs.
- Feel free to use only part of a solution, or combine solutions, to create a solution that will meet your unique needs.

The important thing is that you take action.

Remember, "Without action, we have nothing"—Center for Talent Retention.

Web Links
You'll find a number of the solutions in each manager capability have supporting worksheets to help you complete the solutions. Some of the worksheets will be an Adobe PDF file, and others will be a Microsoft Word template to enable you to enter information directly into the worksheet.

If a solution has a worksheet, the solution's instructions will indicate the page number of the worksheet, as well as provide a web link to download an electronic copy of the worksheet.

The Manager Role

Roles and Responsibilities

All managers have a number of roles and responsibilities. Managers must create business plans, define and administer policies, make decisions, manage a budget, and communicate important information (we know this list is really a mile long).

However, one of the most critical roles any manager has to perform is to engage and retain employees. If a manager is not able to engage team members <u>and</u> keep them from leaving, it would be impossible to achieve the desired team and organization results.

What Do Managers Do?

So what do managers do to engage and retain employee talent?

The Center for Talent Retention conducted an extensive review of the turnover research, case studies, employee satisfaction surveys, performed individual interviews, and facilitated focus groups to identify the actions managers take to impact employee engagement and retention. After reviewing all the data, we found it all came down to 20 distinct manager actions and qualities.

Although these actions do not cover everything a manager is responsible for, they do embody the most critical manager actions needed to <u>engage and retain employee talent</u>.

20 Manager Actions and Qualities

On the following pages you will find each manager action and quality. There are 15 manager actions (manager behaviors) and 5 manager qualities (manager characteristics).

Each of the 5 manager qualities is influenced by one or more of the manager actions. For example, a manager is trusted and respected by employees (a manager quality) because he or she "walks-the-talk", "supports employees during difficult situations", and is a "role model for handling pressure situations". Thus, the quality of "I trust and respect my manager" is achieved as a result of the actions the manager takes.

7 Manager Capabilities

Each of the 15 manager actions fit into one of 7 manager capabilities. These capabilities represent the actions <u>all</u> managers must take on-the-job to engage and retain employee talent. Even though each manager may have his or her own style of managing employees, each of these capabilities is critical for all managers and can be demonstrated through a variety of managerial styles.

Managers Impact Talent Results

Managers communicate with employees, support their work, coach performance, care about them as individuals, establish credibility, provide feedback, and impact talent through their personal actions.

Managers impact engaging and retaining employee talent through seven manager capabilities. These capabilities are further defined into distinct manager actions describing what you would see a manager do on-the-job to impact talent results.

Capability	Action
Coaching Performance	Provide direction and coaching to help employees perform
Supporting Work	Offer the resources and support employees need to be successful
Providing Feedback	Deliver frequent and specific feedback to help employees improve their performance
Establishing Credibility	Role model words and actions that build credibility with others
Show Caring	Take action to show your employees you care about them as individuals
Communication	Create an environment to encourage comfortable two-way dialogue and the exchanging of ideas
Personal Actions	Manage the way you handle difficult and frustrating situations

Manager Actions and Qualities

Below are the 15 manager actions and 5 manager qualities needed to engage and retain employee talent. Each of the 15 manager actions fit into one of 7 manager capabilities. These capabilities are required for <u>all</u> managers to engage and retain employee talent.

7 Manager Capabilities	15 Manager Actions			
Communication	#18 I feel comfortable asking my manager questions and discussing important issues.	#26 My manager actively listens to me and seeks to understand my point of view.	#32 My manager often asks for my ideas.	#40 My manager gets the facts before making judgments or taking action.
Supporting Work	#2 My manager stands up and supports me.	#10 My manager gives me the space I need to do my work.	#20 My manager understands my work.	
Credibility	#22 My manager tells the truth no matter what.	#34 My manager "walks-the-talk".		
Coaching Performance	#28 My goals & performance expectations are clear—I know what it takes to be successful here.	#30 I get a lot of coaching from my manager and other knowledgeable resources.		
Providing Feedback	#14 My manager gives me feedback in private.	#24 My manager gives great feedback—I always know where I stand.		
Caring	#12 My manager genuinely cares about me as a person.			
Personal Actions	#16 My manager knows how to handle personal frustrations.			

5 Manager Qualities					
	#4 I feel comfortable around my manager.	#6 I trust and respect my manager.	#8 My manager is highly qualified.	#36 I really like my manager.	#38 My manager and I have similar personal values.

Building Skills and Capabilities

4 Key Development Questions

Improving your ability to perform the critical manager actions needed to engage and retain employees can be easy. However, before you begin it is important to answer the 4 Key Development Questions.

Question #1 *Do you want to develop?*

Do you want to develop? Seems like a simple question, but it lies at the heart of the issue. Have you made the choice to put forth effort, change the way you do things, and make time for your personal development?

Question #2 *What area of your performance will you develop?*

If you are going to improve, what performance area will you develop? Will you focus on a weakness and consciously try to improve one of your soft points? Will you build a "new capability"? or Will you try to leverage a current strength?

Question #3 *How will you develop your capabilities?*

To become proficient in any of the manager capabilities we recommend a performance-based development process. This type of development is built on the premise—*people "develop-by-doing"*. Performance-based development requires you to take action in your current role using structured processes and experiences.

The *FAST* Action Development Guide provides performance-based development actions for each manager capability.

Question #4 *What's your development plan?*

Someone once said, "Not creating a plan, is planning to fail". This holds true for development. It is absolutely critical for you to identify what you will do to improve your capabilities. General development may happen over time, but targeted development rarely happens without a solid plan.

Successful development plans are simple. They define what area will be developed and how development will occur. The *FAST* Action Development Guide will walk you through the steps needed to select an area to develop, choose actions from multiple development options, and assess the impact of your actions.

Developing Your Capabilities

The following actions will help you identify a manager capability to develop, select the development actions to implement, and monitor your development progress.

Evaluate Your Strengths and Weaknesses
Evaluate your current performance on the critical manager actions with a self-assessment or by obtaining feedback from others.

Self-Assessment
Evaluate your individual performance to identify your strengths and weaknesses
Use the Assessment Processes to determine how well you perform the critical manager actions impacting employee engagement and retention.

Your self-assessment results will be as good as you make them. You will have to reflect on what others have said about your performance, reactions you generate with your interactions, and what reputation you have really earned to accurately assess your performance.

Performance Feedback
Obtain performance feedback from others
Use the Assessment Processes to receive feedback on your performance from others (e.g., your employees, manager, and/or peers).

It is critical to let your assessors know you desire an accurate picture of your strengths and weaknesses. Share your desire to improve your personal capabilities, and explain how you will use their feedback to help you select what area to develop first.

Assessing Your Capabilities

The Assessment Processes

Below you will find two assessment processes. The first assessment, the Retention Cards™ Assessment, uses a tool called the Retention Cards™ to evaluate individual performance (for more information on the Retention Cards™ visit www.keeppeople.com). If you do not have a set of the Retention Cards™, you can use the *Manager Action Check Sheet* to evaluate your performance.

Retention Cards™ Assessment

Use the Retention Cards™ to perform a self-assessment or obtain performance feedback from others to understand your current level of performance on the critical manager actions.

Manager Action Check Sheet

The Manager Action Check Sheet can be used (without the Retention Cards™) to perform a self-assessment or obtain performance feedback from others to understand your current level of performance on the critical manager actions.

Retention Cards™ Assessment

Retention Cards™ Assessment
Use the Retention Cards™ to perform a self-assessment or obtain performance feedback from others.

Step 1
Preparation
- Select the 20 Manager Action cards from the Retention Cards™ deck (each card will have an "M" in the top right corner)
- Select the Blue Header cards labeled (D) A Weakness, (E) Average, and (F) A Strength
- Make a copy of the *Manager Actions Assessment* worksheet for yourself and/or anyone else who will be giving you feedback
   Download electronic copy: www.keeppeople.com/book/mgrassessment.pdf

Step 2
Perform the Sort Process
The purpose of the sort process is to sort the cards into three piles based on your current performance. To sort the cards, read the "green" side of each Manager Action card and determine if it is a strength, an average capability, or a weakness. Place the card next to the corresponding blue header card.

It is important to note this is a **forced sort**. You must place only 6 cards in the *A Strength* pile, 8 cards in the *Average* pile, and 6 cards in the *A Weakness* pile.

Use the following definitions to help sort the cards.

A Weakness (6 Cards)
Your weakest capabilities—actions you perform poorly or which need improvement

Average (8 cards)
Your average capabilities—actions you perform well and have received satisfactory feedback

A Strength (6 cards)
Your greatest strengths—actions you are very good at and are known for your excellent skills in these areas

Step 3
Summarize the Results
Use the *Manager Actions Assessment* worksheet to summarize your results from your self-assessment or performance feedback. Place an "S", "A", or "W" in the upper right-hand box in each manager action and quality to indicate your strengths, average capabilities, and weaknesses.

Manager Actions Assessment

Step 1
Place an "S", "A", or "W" in the upper right-hand box in each manager action and quality to indicate your strengths, average capabilities, and weaknesses.

Step 2
Review your areas of strengths, average capabilities, and weaknesses in each manager capability.
- Which capability needs the most attention?
- Which capability, if developed, would have the greatest impact on engaging and retaining your employee talent?

Step C
Focus your development efforts by selecting one manager capability to develop for the next 90 days.

7 Manager Capabilities	15 Manager Actions			
Communication	#18 I feel comfortable asking my manager questions and discussing important issues.	#26 My manager actively listens to me and seeks to understand my point of view.	#32 My manager often asks for my ideas.	#40 My manager gets the facts before making judgments or taking action.
Supporting Work	#2 My manager stands up and supports me.	#10 My manager gives me the space I need to do my work.	#20 My manager understands my work.	
Credibility	#22 My manager tells the truth no matter what.	#34 My manager "walks-the-talk".		
Coaching Performance	#28 My goals & performance expectations are clear—I know what it takes to be successful here.	#30 I get a lot of coaching from my manager and other knowledgeable resources.		
Providing Feedback	#14 My manager gives me feedback in private.	#24 My manager gives great feedback—I always know where I stand.		
Caring	#12 My manager genuinely cares about me as a person.			
Personal Actions	#16 My manager knows how to handle personal frustrations.			
5 Manager Qualities	#4 I feel comfortable around my manager.	#6 I trust and respect my manager.	#8 My manager is highly qualified.	#36 I really like my manager.	#38 My manager and I have similar personal values.

Download electronic copy: www.keeppeople.com/book/mgrassessment.pdf

Manager Assessment

Manager Action Check Sheet

Use the *Manager Action Check Sheet* to perform a self-assessment or obtain performance feedback from others.

Step 1
Preparation
- Make a copy of the *Manager Action Check Sheet*
    Download electronic copy: **www.keeppeople.com/book/checksheet.pdf**
- Make a copy of the *Manager Actions Assessment* worksheet for yourself and/or anyone else who will be giving you feedback
    Download electronic copy: **www.keeppeople.com/book/mgrassessment.pdf**

Step 2
Complete the Manager Action Check Sheet

Read through <u>all</u> 15 actions statements below before you begin. Based on your observations and experiences, identify the person's strengths, average capabilities, and weaknesses. Mark 5 statements as *A Strength*, 5 as *Average*, and 5 as *A Weakness*. Mark *NA* if the statement does not "fit" the person's accountabilities.

Step 3
Summarize the Results

Use the *Manager Actions Assessment* worksheet to summarize your results from your self-assessment or performance feedback. Place an "S", "A", or "W" in the upper right-hand box in each manager action and quality to indicate your strengths, average capabilities, and weaknesses.

Manager Action Check Sheet

Read through <u>all</u> 15 actions statements below before you begin. Based on your observations and experiences, identify the person's strengths, average capabilities, and weaknesses. Mark 5 statements as *A Strength*, 5 as *Average*, and 5 as *A Weakness*. Mark *NA* if the statement does not "fit" the person's accountabilities.

Note: The term "Manager" is used to describe a person who has management responsibilities. The person's title may be team leader, director, coach, project leader, or supervisor.

7 Manager Capabilities	Action Statements (The Employee Viewpoint—What employees would say)	5 Strength	5 Average	5 Weakness	NA
Communication	I feel comfortable asking my manager questions and discussing important issues.	○	○	○	○
	My manager actively listens to me and seeks to understand my point of view.	○	○	○	○
	My manager often asks for my ideas.	○	○	○	○
	My manager gets the facts before making judgments or taking action.	○	○	○	○
Supporting Work	My manager stands up and supports me.	○	○	○	○
	My manager gives me the space I need to do my work.	○	○	○	○
	My manager understands my work.	○	○	○	○
Credibility	My manager tells the truth no matter what.	○	○	○	○
	My manager "walks-the-talk".	○	○	○	○
Feedback	My manager gives me feedback in private.	○	○	○	○
	My manager gives great feedback—I always know where I stand.	○	○	○	○
Coaching Performance	My goals & performance expectations are clear—I know what it takes to be successful here.	○	○	○	○
	I get a lot of coaching from my manager and other knowledgeable resources.	○	○	○	○
Caring	My manager genuinely cares about me as a person.	○	○	○	○
Personal Actions	My manager knows how to handle personal frustrations.	○	○	○	○
	Total for Each Column				

Download electronic copy:
www.keeppeople.com/book/checksheet.pdf

Create Your Development Plan

The following steps will help you complete your development plan.

Step 1
Choose Development Actions to Implement
- Review the development actions listed for the manager capability you selected.
- Read the detailed action steps <u>and</u> review the associated worksheets.
- Select the development actions that best fit your personal situation and check the actions off on the manager capability overview page.

*Be sure to pick at least one development action in each time frame (48 Hours, 7 Days, 30 Days, and 90 Days).

Step 2
Prepare to Develop

Review the detailed instructions of the development actions you have selected and download copies of the worksheets you will need to implement the development actions. Using your PDA, on-line calendar, or day-timer, schedule the actions you must take to complete the 48 Hour and 7 Day development actions.

Step 3
Take Action

At the end of your work week summarize the actions you actually implemented, and review your next development actions (7 days, 30 days, and 90 days) and schedule these actions in your calendar.

Step 4
Celebrate

Be sure to celebrate the progress you achieve throughout your development journey!

Go to Your Manager Capability

Coaching Performance
Page 19

Supporting Work
Page 55

Providing Feedback
Page 89

Establishing Credibility
Page 123

Show Caring
Page 157

Communication
Page 191

Personal Actions
Page 225

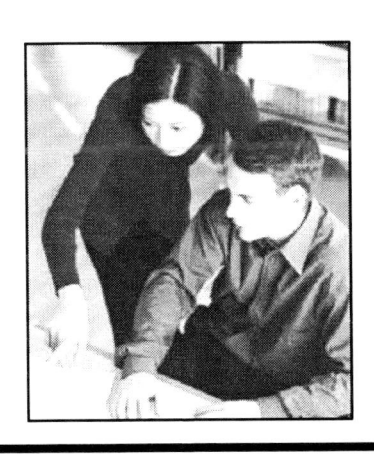

Coaching Performance

Provide direction and coaching to help employees perform

Coaching Performance

48 Hours

1.1 Talk-it-Up!
Tell your manager, team, and peers you plan to improve your "coaching" skills

1.2 Benefit Analysis
Determine whether improving your coaching skills will be valuable for yourself and others

1.3 Coaching Time
Create regularly scheduled coaching time for team members

1.4 Stand-Up Huddles
Meet daily with your team to check progress, clarify direction, and refocus efforts

7 Days

1.5 Two 4 U: Ideas for Improvement
Ask others for two ideas to improve your coaching skills

1.6 Tracking Chart
Create a tracking chart to capture your coaching progress

1.7 Coaching Actions
Determine the top actions you will take to help your employees

1.8 Coaching Network
Help each employee identify a team of coaching resources

1.9 Team Action Profile
Outline what team members must do to deliver high performing results

30 Days

1.10 Team Discussion
Facilitate a team discussion to improve your coaching skills

1.11 Feedback for Me
Receive feedback on your coaching actions

1.12 Project Coaching
Identify coaching opportunities within your team members' current projects

1.13 SMART Objectives
Create individual performance objectives for the team and each employee

1.14 Team Goal Calibration
Ensure each team member is focused on the deliverables needed to achieve your desired team results

90 Days

1.15 Mini-Assessment
Assess your coaching performance progress

1.16 Bust-up the Roadblocks
Identify the obstacles and hurdles preventing you from improving your coaching skills

1.17 Role Discussion
Review each team member's role and responsibilities

1.18 Team Member Development Plan
Create a development plan with your team members

1.19 Team Goal Grid
Show how each team member contributes to the team goals

Coaching Performance
48 Hours

Prep Time
5 minutes

Action Time
15 minutes

1.1
Talk-it-Up!
Tell your manager, team, and peers you plan to improve your coaching skills

Identify the individuals and/or groups who will be most impacted by a change in your coaching skills and share your desire to improve your capabilities.

Step 1: In a team meeting, share your desire to improve your coaching capabilities. Be sure to discuss the following:
- Explain "why" you have chosen to improve your coaching skills
- Describe how an increase in performance will help you, the organization, and others
- Outline what you actions you plan to take to impact your capabilities

Step 2: Solicit the groups' help and feedback. Ask them to support your development by focusing on your coaching actions from this point forward (not what you did in the past). Ask them to give you feedback on what you are doing well and what you need to improve.

Note: *Talk-it-Up!* is best done face-to-face, however, you can also *Talk-it-Up!* during a conference call or via email.

Coaching Performance
48 Hours

Prep Time 5 minutes   *Action Time* 10 minutes

Download electronic copy:
www.keeppeople.com/book/1.2.dot

1.2
Benefit Analysis
Determine whether improving your coaching skills will be valuable for yourself and others

Complete a *Benefit Analysis* to determine whether improving your coaching skills will be valuable for yourself and others.

Step 1: Identify the key individuals and/or groups who will be most impacted by a change in your coaching skills. Record their names on the **Benefit Analysis Square** (page 41).

Step 2: For each individual or group, answer the following question:

"If you improve your coaching capabilities, what benefits will be experienced by the individual or group?"

Identify two benefits for each individual or group, and record your responses on the *Benefit Analysis Square*.

Step 3: After completing the *Benefit Analysis Square*, determine whether the benefits of improving your coaching capabilities outweigh the time and energy needed to improve your performance.

- If YES, move forward and take action to improve your coaching capabilities
- If NO, select another manager capability to improve

Example

Your Employees
1. My coaching time will show I care about their personal development.
2. I will make time to ensure each person knows exactly what he or she must do to be successful.

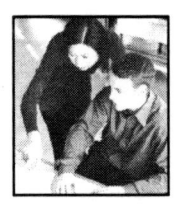

Coaching Performance
48 Hours

Prep Time **10 minutes** *Action Time* **TBD**

1.3
Coaching Time
Create regularly scheduled coaching time for team members

Create and post dedicated time slots each week for team members to clarify expectations, discuss priorities, ask questions, and clarify next steps.

Step 1: Share the purpose of the *Coaching Time* with your team.

Step 2: Post your *Coaching Time* slots on your door, work space, or on an on-line calendar (e.g., Monday 2—4 p.m.).

Step 3: Team members should be able to schedule time within the *Coaching Time*, or be able to stop by your desk if you do not have a scheduled meeting with another team member.

Note:
- Be sure to hold your "Coaching Time" sacred. Team members should know you are always available during your dedicated coaching times.

- You may also want to request a discussion with a team member during the *Coaching Time* to share new information, make changes in objectives, or receive a status update.

Coaching Performance
48 Hours

Prep Time 10 minutes   *Action Time* 5 minutes

1.4
Stand-Up Huddles
Meet daily with your team to check progress, clarify direction, and refocus efforts

Share critical information impacting team member's priorities and/or team goals.

Step 1: Select a time each day (mornings are best) to conduct a 5 minute Priority Huddle.

Step 2: At each Priority Huddle, share the critical information impacting the priorities of the team and/or team member goals. This information should help team members make any necessary adjustments in their work day to ensure they focus on the critical actions needed for success.

Note:
- It is critical you stick to the time limit. If needed, select an individual to hold the group accountable to 5 minutes.
- If needed, problem solving should follow the Priority Huddle, and should only include the people who need to be involved.

Coaching Performance
7 Days

Prep Time **5 minutes**

Action Time **60 minutes**

Download electronic copy:
www.keeppeople.com/book/1.5.dot

1.5
Two 4 U: Ideas for Improvement
Ask others for two ideas to improve your coaching skills

Using the wisdom and experience from others, generate as many ideas as possible to improve your coaching capabilities.

Step 1: Identify up to 5 people who have excellent coaching skills.

Step 2: Ask each person the following question:

"I'm trying to improve my coaching skills, do you have two ideas for how I can improve my capabilities?"

Step 3: Record each person's ideas on the **Two 4 U** worksheet (page 42).

Step 4: Once you gathered ideas from each person, review the suggestions and circle the top three ideas you think will help the most.

Step 5: For your top three ideas, identify the next steps you will take to implement the idea.

Step 6: Thank the individuals who gave you the development ideas and share what actions you plan to take to improve your coaching capabilities.

Coaching Performance
7 Days

Prep Time **5 minutes**

Action Time **10 minutes**

Download electronic copy:
www.keeppeople.com/book/1.6.dot

1.6
Tracking Chart
Create a tracking chart to capture your coaching progress

Each Friday capture what you actually completed during the week to improve your coaching skills.

Step 1: Each Friday, identify and record the actions you took to improve your performance on the **Tracking Chart** (page 43).

Step 2: For each action, grade your performance based on how well you think you performed on the action, as well as considering feedback you may have received from others.

A = Excellent; B = Good; C = Average; D = Poor; F = Failing

Step 3: Based on your performance, identify one improvement action you will implement the following week.

Step 4: After completing the *Tracking Chat* ask yourself the following questions:
- Am I really taking actions to improve?
- Are my actions having the desired impact on my coaching capabilities?

Example

Week	Coaching Actions	Grade
August 14	Gave performance feedback to Kathy	C
	Identified a budget management resource for Caroline	A
	Outlined performance expectations with Jim for Project X	B
Improvement Actions • Schedule time with Kathy to create a Coaching Network		

Coaching Performance
7 Days

Prep Time
5 minutes

Action Time
15 minutes/ employee

Download electronic copy:
www.keeppeople.com/book/1.7.dot

1.7
Coaching Actions
Determine the top coaching actions you will take to help your employees

Conduct a 15 minute discussion with each team member to identify one coaching action you can take to help the employee be successful in his or her role.

Step 1: Identify a block of time you can meet with your team members over the next two weeks—plan for 15 minutes per employee. Post these time blocks outside your door, on an on-line calendar, or in a general meeting area.

Step 2: Send the following email to your team, or introduce the "Coaching Actions" in a team meeting.

As you know, I am working on improving my coaching capabilities. To understand what coaching actions would be helpful to you, I'd like to have a quick 15 minute discussion with each of you in the next two weeks. During this discussion, we will identify one coaching action I can take to help you achieve your deliverables, build your capabilities, or provide you with better feedback.
   Before we meet, I need some help from you...
   1. *Please schedule yourself for a 15 minute discussion on the posted schedule located (insert location) within the next two days.*
   2. *Be prepared to discuss what coaching actions you believe will help you achieve your deliverables, build your capabilities, or create a greater understanding of your current performance.*

During the discussion, we'll review your current needs and identify one coaching action I can take to help you be successful.

Step 3: Meet with each team member and discuss the team member's coaching needs. Identify the top coaching action you will take for the employee and record the action on the **Coaching Actions** worksheet (page 44).

Step 4: Follow-up with each team member to identify how the coaching action helped the employee. Determine if additional coaching actions may be needed to ensure the employee is successful in his or her role.

Example

Employee	Action	Completed	
Chris	Schedule bi-weekly feedback sessions	☑	Date 5/1
Tom	Identify an expert in candidate selection to act as a resource	☑	Date 5/30

Coaching Performance
7 Days

Prep Time
5 minutes

Action Time
15 minutes/ employee

Download electronic copy:
www.keeppeople.com/book/1.8.dot

1.8
Coaching Network
Help each employee identify a team of coaching resources

With your team members, create a *Coaching Network* of individuals who will be able to provide coaching and performance feedback on the skills and capabilities team members would like to develop.

Step 1: With each team member, identify the skills and capabilities the team member would like to build over the next 12 months.

Step 2: Based on the skills and capabilities the team member would like to build, identify two individuals who can provide coaching to the team member on at least one of the identified skills and capabilities.

Step 3: Record the names of the individuals on the **Coaching Network** worksheet (page 45), identifying the specific area skill or capability the individual can provide the team member coaching on.

Step 4: Team members should solicit help when needed, and schedule dedicated time to receive direct coaching from the individuals within his or her Coaching Network.

Coaching Performance
7 Days

Prep Time
60 minutes

Action Time
TBD

1.9
Team Action Profile
Outline what team members must do to deliver high performing results

Facilitate a team discussion to create an "Action Profile" that outlines what team members must do (day-to-day, week-to-week) to deliver "high performing results".

Step 1: In a team meeting, discuss the team's performance by using the questions below to create a clear picture of the team's current performance.
- What results has the team achieved?
- What results were NOT delivered?
- If an outsider observed the team for a week, what actions would this person see?
- On a scale of 1 to 10 (1 = "we're the worst we can be"; 10 = "we're the best we can be"), how would you rate the team's current performance?

Step 2: Based on the team's current performance, identify the actions all team members must take in the following areas to deliver high performing results:

Start: What actions do team members need to start doing?
(e.g., *Provide weekly project status updates*)

Stop: What actions do team members need to stop doing?
(e.g., *Arriving for and starting meetings late*)

Continue: What actions do team members need to continue doing?
(e.g., *Recognizing each other's good work*)

Step 3: Review the "Action Profile" periodically (in meetings, conference calls, etc.) to highlight the teams' consistency with the actions needed to deliver high performing results.

Coaching Performance
30 Days

Prep Time **5 minutes**   *Action Time* **45 minutes**

1.10
Team Discussion
Facilitate a team discussion to improve your coaching skills

Solicit ideas from your team to improve your coaching capabilities, and identify a way to receive immediate feedback as you implement your coaching actions.

Step 1: In a team meeting share "why" you want to improve your coaching skills, and share your thoughts about the importance of coaching performance.

Step 2: Ask your team members to share how they think your coaching capabilities impact the team and individual team members.

Step 3: Ask the team to brainstorm actions you can take to improve your coaching skills.

Step 4: With the team, identify a way for team members to cue you when your actions are consistent, as well as inconsistent with the desired coaching behaviors.

Try pick two hand gestures, statements, or signals to indicate when the new coaching behaviors are happening and when they're not.

For example, team members may say *"Right on Coach!"* when your behaviors are consistent, and *"Tale a step back Coach"* when your behaviors are inconsistent. Teams members may also use a hand gesture such as "thumbs-up" or "thumbs-down".

Coaching Performance
30 Days

Prep Time
5 minutes

Action Time
2 hours

Download electronic copy:
www.keeppeople.com/book/1.11.dot

1.11
Feedback for Me
Receive feedback on your coaching actions

Solicit feedback on the actions you have taken to improve your coaching capabilities.

Step 1: Identify up to 5 people who can give you feedback on your coaching actions, and send them the following email:

> *I have chosen to take action to improve my coaching skills and would like some help from you. In the next 30 to 45 days, I'd like to follow-up with you to receive feedback on my "coaching" performance. When we talk, I will ask you the following questions:*
> 1. *What coaching actions have you seen me perform?*
> 2. *What impact have my actions created for individuals, the team, and/or the organization?*
> 3. *What improvement ideas do you have for me?*
>
> *Thank you for your help. I look forward to speaking with you soon.*

Step 2: Identify a follow-up date when you will ask each person for feedback. Record the date on the **Feedback for Me** worksheet (page 46).

Step 3: At the time of your follow-up dates, schedule a 15 minute discussion with each person to receive feedback on your coaching actions.

Step 4: After receiving feedback, record the feedback on the *Feedback for Me* worksheet. Be sure to thank each person for his or her time and willingness to provide you feedback on your coaching actions.

Step 5: Based on the feedback you received, think about the following:
- What coaching actions do I need to do more of?
- What actions do I need to do less of?
- What additional actions should I integrate into my coaching improvement plan?

Coaching Performance
30 Days

Prep Time
5 minutes

Action Time
45 minutes/ employee

Download electronic copy:
www.keeppeople.com/book/1.12.dot

1.12
Project Coaching
Identify coaching opportunities within your team members' current projects

Meet with each team member to determine if the team member's current project and deliverables provide the opportunity to build new skills and capabilities.

Step 1: Meet with each team member to review his or her current projects. Use the **Project Coaching** worksheet (page 47) to identify the following:
- What are the team member's current projects?
- What skills and capabilities are needed to successfully complete the projects?
- What is the team member's current performance level on the required skills and capabilities?
- Are there opportunities for developing new skills or capabilities?

Step 2: Based on the team member's current projects, determine how the team member can leverage his or her current projects to develop new skills or capabilities.

Step 3: Together, identify the actions both you and the team member need to take to use the team member's current projects to provide development opportunities.

Coaching Performance
30 Days

Prep Time **15 minutes**　　*Action Time* **45 minutes**

Download electronic copy:
www.keeppeople.com/book/1.13.dot

1.13
SMART Objectives
Create individual performance objectives for the team and each employee

Work with your team members to create SMART objectives that outline what they must deliver in the next year.

Step 1: In a team meeting give each team member the **SMART Objectives** worksheet (page 48) and describe the following process:
  A. Each team member will work on the worksheet to outline what they must deliver in the next year.
  B. Using the instructions on the worksheet, each objective must meet the SMART criteria.
  C. You and each team member will meet to review the worksheet and make any necessary upgrades.

Step 2: Schedule a time to meet with each team member or have peers work together to help each other shape up the objectives.

Step 3: During the meeting perform the following:
- <u>Review</u> the team member's SMART objectives and determine if the objectives are the right ones based on the individual's role. Some objectives may need to be modified or deleted, or you may want to add additional deliverables.
- <u>Shape up</u> the objectives so that each meets the SMART criteria.

Step 4: Identify and share the actions you can take to help the team member successfully achieve his or her objectives.

Step 5: Periodically touch base with your team member to review his or her objectives and make any necessary upgrades to reflect changing team and business priorities.

Coaching Performance
30 Days

Prep Time **10 minutes** *Action Time* **2 hours**

1.14
Team Goal Calibration
Ensure each team member is focused on the deliverables needed to achieve your desired team results

Facilitate a 1 to 2 hour Team Calibration Session to ensure each team member is focused on the deliverables and actions needed to achieve your desired team results.

Before the Session:
Step 1: Outline what your team must deliver in the next 3 to 6 months to achieve your desired team results.

Step 2: Ask each team member to identify what he or she must deliver over the next 3 to 6 months to achieve their individual performance objectives.

Step 3: Create a Team Goal Network on a flip chart or dry erase board.

During the Session:
Step 4: Review the team deliverables on the Team Goal Network.

Step 5: Have each team member record their individual deliverables under the goal the deliverable supports.

Step 6: Use the following questions to facilitate a team discussion:
- Will the team goals be reached if all the team member's deliverables are achieved?
- Do additional actions need to be added to achieve the team goals?
- Are team members delivering the right actions based on their role, skills, and capabilities?

Example

Team Members	Goal #1: Increase team size by 20%	Goal #2: Increase customer base by 10%
John	Select 10 candidates to interview by 9/30	N/A
Sarah	Interview 3 candidates by 10/15	Create marketing plan by 9/1

Coaching Performance
90 Days

Prep Time **10 minutes** *Action Time* **30 minutes**

Download electronic copy:
www.keeppeople.com/book/1.15.pdf

1.15
Mini-Assessment
Assess your coaching performance progress

Determine if your coaching actions are perceived as more effective.

45 Days Before the Mini-Assessment:
Step 1: Identify the individuals and/or groups who will be most impacted by a change in your coaching capabilities and share your desire to improve your coaching skills.

Step 2: Explain "why" you have chosen to improve your coaching capabilities. Describe how an increase in performance will help you, the organization, and others.

Step 3: Solicit their help and feedback. Ask the individuals to support your development by observing your actions for 45 days. Tell them at the end of the 45 days you will give them a *Mini-Assessment* to evaluate your coaching actions.

The Mini-Assessment:
Step 4: After 45 days, give a copy of the **Mini-Assessment** (page 49) to the individuals you asked to observe your behaviors—ask them to complete the *Mini-Assessment* honestly.

Step 5: Request the individuals return the assessment to you when they are finished.

Step 6: Summarize your results for each statement. Where do you have strengths and weaknesses?

Step 7: Identify actions you will take based on your *Mini-Assessment* results.

Step 8: Share these actions with the individuals who gave you feedback and thank them for their help.

Coaching Performance
90 Days

Prep Time **5 minutes** *Action Time* **15 minutes**

Download electronic copy:
www.keeppeople.com/book/1.16.dot

1.16
Bust-up the Roadblocks
Identify the obstacles and hurdles preventing you from improving your coaching skills

Identify why you may not be taking action to improve your coaching skills, and/or determine why the actions you have taken are not having the desired impact.

Step 1: Record your current and planned coaching actions on the **Bust-up the Roadblocks** (page 50) worksheet.

Step 2: Review each action and determine if a "roadblock" or obstacle is preventing you from implementing a planned action or preventing a current action from creating its desired impact.

Step 3: Based on the "roadblock", identify "bust-up" actions you can take to eliminate or manage the roadblock.

Example

Current and Planned Coaching Actions	"Roadblock" or Obstacle	"Bust-up" Action
I plan to perform a One-to-One Dialogue with each team member in the next 6 weeks.	I don't have the time to meet with all my team members for a One-to-One Dialogue within the next 6 weeks.	In the next 6 weeks I will meet with team members who are at risk of disengaging from their work or leaving the team. Once I meet with these team members, I'll schedule additional One-to-One Dialogues.

Coaching Performance
90 Days

Prep Time
10 minutes/ employee

Action Time
45 minutes/ employee

Download electronic copy:
www.keeppeople.com/book/1.17.dot

1.17
Role Discussion
Review each team member's role and responsibilities

Conduct a 30 to 60 minute discussion with each team member to review the individual's current role and responsibilities.

Before the discussion:

Step 1: Schedule a time with the team member to conduct a *Role Review*.

Step 2: Outline what you think the team member's role and responsibilities are.

During the discussion:

Step 3: Ask the employee to describe his or her current role and responsibilities.

Step 4: Identify any gaps between what you think the team member's role requires, and what the team member thinks his or her role requires.

Step 5: Determine if there are responsibilities that need to be added, deleted, or modified within the team member's role.

Step 6: Capture the updated role description and responsibilities on the **Role Review** Worksheet (page 51).

Coaching Performance
90 Days

Prep Time
10 minutes/ employee

Action Time
45 minutes/ employee

Download electronic copy:
www.keeppeople.com/book/1.18.dot

1.18
Team Member Development Plan
Create a development plan with your team members

Work with your team members to create a Team Member Development Plan outlining the skills and capabilities they need to achieve their individual performance objectives.

Step 1: Schedule a time to meet with each team member.

Step 2: During the meeting, work with your team member to complete a **Team Member Development Plan** (page 52) and outline the following:
- What individual goals and work priorities does the team member need to deliver?
- What are the team member's development interests?
- What skills and capabilities does the team member need to achieve his or her individual goals?

Step 3: Based on the answers to the questions above, identify the development actions the team member should implement over the next year.

Step 4: Identify the actions both you and the team member must take to ensure the team member is able to successfully implement the selected development actions.

Note: Be sure to check your plan…if the team member completes the development actions, will they increase his or her capability to perform?

Coaching Performance
90 Days

Prep Time: **15 minutes** Action Time: **2 hours**

1.19
Team Goal Grid
Show how each team member contributes to the team goals

Create and post a Team Goal Grid showing how each team member contributes to the most important team goals and deliverables.

Step 1: In a team meeting, use a flip chart or dry erase board to create a *Team Goal Grid*. Use the *Team Goal Grid* to record the critical goals and deliverables the team must achieve in the next 6 to 12 months. Record each team members' name on the *Team Goal Grid*.

Step 3: Team members should review the team goals and deliverables and determine what actions and results they will deliver to support the team goals. Team members record the action or deliverable in their row on the *Team Goal Grid*.

Note: Team members may or may not contribute to every goal.

Step 4: With your team, review each team goal or deliverable on the *Team Goal Grid* and discuss the following:
- If each team member delivered his or her identified actions and results, would the team goal or deliverable be achieved at a high level of performance?
- Are there additional actions or results needed to deliver the team goal at a high level of performance?
- Are there team members who are "spread too thin" across the deliverables?
- Are there team members who need to add additional results or actions?

Note:
- Additional time may be required to resolve some issues uncovered during the *Team Goal Grid* process.
- Team members may need one-to-one coaching with you to ensure each team member is accountable for the right actions and results.

Example

Team Members	Goal #1: Project ALPHA	Goal #2: Increase team size by 25%
Fred	N/A	Select 8 candidates to interview by 1/10
Debbie	Functionality A and B by 4/1	Interview 3 candidates by 2/1

Coaching Performance

1.2
Benefit Analysis Square

For each individual or group, answer the following question:

"If you improve your coaching capabilities, what benefits will be experienced by the individual or group?"

Identify two benefits for each individual or group, and record your responses below.

Determine whether the benefits of improving your coaching capabilities outweigh the time and energy needed to improve your performance.

- If YES, move forward and take action to improve your coaching capabilities
- If NO, select another manager capability to improve

Yourself	Your Manager	Your Employees
1.	1.	1.
2.	2.	2.

Your Peers & Co-Workers	**Benefits**	Key Customers & Clients
1.		1.
2.		2.

Your Significant Other/Family	Other _____	Other _____
1.	1.	1.
2.	2.	2.

COACHING PERFORMANCE

1.5
Two 4 U

Identify up to 5 people who have excellent coaching skills and ask each person the following question:

"I'm trying to improve my coaching skills, do you have two ideas for how I can improve my capabilities?"

Record each person's ideas below. Once you gathered ideas from each person, review the suggestions and circle the top three ideas you think will help the most.

For your top three ideas, identify the next steps you will take to implement the idea.

Individual	Idea #1	Idea #2	Next Steps

Coaching Performance

1.6
Tracking Chart

Each Friday, identify and record the actions you took to improve your performance. For each action, grade your performance based on how well you think you performed on the action, as well as considering feedback you may have received from others.

A = Excellent; B = Good; C = Average; D = Poor; F = Failing

Based on your performance, identify one improvement action you will implement the following week.

Week	Coaching Actions	Grade

Improvement Action:

Week	Coaching Actions	Grade

Improvement Action:

Week	Coaching Actions	Grade

Improvement Action:

Coaching Performance

1.7
Coaching Actions

Meet with each team member and discuss the team member's coaching needs. Identify the top coaching action you will take for the employee and record the action below.

When you complete the action, record the date and mark it complete.

Employee	Action	Completed
		☐ Date:
		☐ Date:
		☐ Date:
		☐ Date:
		☐ Date:
		☐ Date:
		☐ Date:
		☐ Date:
		☐ Date:
		☐ Date:
		☐ Date:
		☐ Date:
		☐ Date:
		☐ Date:

Coaching Performance

1.8
Coaching Network

Record the names of the individuals who can provide coaching to the team member, as well as the skill or capability they can provide coaching on.

	Coaching Resource #1
Name	
Skill or Capability	
	Coaching Resource #2
Name	
Skill or Capability	

Coaching Performance

1.11
Feedback for Me

Identify up to 5 people who can give you feedback on your coaching actions. Determine when you will follow-up with each person and record the date below.

After receiving feedback, record the feedback from each person.

Based on the feedback you received, think about the following:
- What coaching actions do I need to do more of?
- What actions do I need to do less of?
- What additional actions should I integrate into my coaching improvement plan?

Name	Follow-Up Date	Feedback		
		What coaching actions have you seen me perform?	*What impact have my actions created for individuals, the team, and/or the organization?*	*What improvement ideas do you have for me?*

Coaching Performance

1.12
Project Coaching

Answer the questions below to identify how you can leverage your current projects to develop new skills and capabilities.
- What are your current projects?
- What skills and capabilities are needed to successfully complete the projects?
- What is your current performance level on the required skills and capabilities?
- Are there opportunities for developing new skills or capabilities?

Team Member:
Date:

Current Projects	Needed Skills and Capabilities	Current Performance	Development Opportunities

Actions to Leverage Development Opportunities

Coaching Performance

1.13
SMART Objectives

Think about the next year, and identify the goals and work priorities you must deliver. Record your objectives below.

For each objective, determine which of the SMART critiera the objective meets and mark the corresponding letter.

Re-write your objectives until you can check-off each letter.

Team Member:

SMART Criteria

Specific:
- The objective clearly describes what will be accomplished
- The objective states a clear and concise result or outcome

Measurable:
- The objective describes the criteria used to evaluate success (e.g., quantity, quality, speed, productivity, cost, completion)

Attainable:
- The objective is a challenge but within reason for the individual's ability

Relevant:
- The objective applies to the individual's role
- The objective is linked to the team's and/or organization's goals

Time bound:
- The objective states when the deliverable needs to start and/or finish

Individual Performance Objectives	S	M	A	R	T

Coaching Performance

1.15
Mini-Assessment

A little over a month ago I began improving my coaching capabilities. Please help me gauge my performance by taking 5 minutes to answer a few questions. Please return the assessment with the enclosed envelope.

Thank you for your feedback!

Coaching Mini-Assessment

Please evaluate my improvement in the area of coaching.
For each of the following statements, circle the level of change you have noticed in my actions in the last 45 Days.

Am I MORE or LESS effective on the following...

Less Effective	No Perceivable Change	More Effective	Not Applicable
-2 -1	0 +1	+2	NA

I clarify individual goals and performance expectations

-2   -1   0   +1   +2   NA

I set team performance goals and behavior expectations

-2   -1   0   +1   +2   NA

I take actions to help you improve your performance

-2   -1   0   +1   +2   NA

We discuss your performance and ways you can improve

-2   -1   0   +1   +2   NA

I provide coaching time

-2   -1   0   +1   +2   NA

What else can I do to become a more effective coach for you?

_____
_____
_____
_____

Center for Talent Retention © 2000-2005

COACHING PERFORMANCE

1.16
Bust-up the Roadblocks

Record your current and planned coaching actions below. Review each action and determine if a "roadblock" or obstacle is preventing you from implementing a planned action or preventing a current action from creating its desired impact. Based on the "roadblock", identify "bust-up" actions you can take to eliminate or manage the roadblock.

Current and Planned Coaching Actions	"Roadblock" or Obstacle	"Bust-up" Action

Coaching Performance

1.17
Role Discussion
Capture the team member's updated role description and responsibilities below.

Team Member:

Role Description

Current Responsibilities

Coaching Performance

1.18
Team Member Development Plan
Answer the questions below and identify the development actions you will implement over the next year.

Team Member:
Date:

What are your individual goals and work priorities?

What are your development interests?

What skills and capabilities do you need to achieve your individual goals?

Development Actions	Due Date

Supporting Work

Offer the resources and support employees need to be successful

Supporting Work

48 Hours

2.1 Talk-it-Up!
Tell your manager, team, and peers you plan to improve your "supporting work" skills

2.2 Benefit Analysis
Determine whether improving your "supporting work" skills will be valuable for yourself and others

2.3 Project Updates
Create a regularly schedule time slot for team members to give you updates on their work

2.4 Supporting Work Assessment
Evaluate the support you recently provided a team member

7 Days

2.5 Two 4 U: Ideas for Improvement
Ask others for two ideas to improve your "supporting work" skills

2.6 Tracking Chart
Create a tracking chart to capture your "supporting work" progress

2.7 Assess My Support
Ask your employees to evaluate the support you provide them

2.8 Support Grid
Identify actions you will take in the future to increase the level of support you provide others

2.9 Learning from Others
Ask a person who is really good at "supporting work" to give you feedback

30 Days

2.10 Team Discussion
Facilitate a team discussion to improve your "supporting work" skills

2.11 Feedback for Me
Receive feedback on your "supporting work" actions

2.12 Education Session
Spend time with each of your employees to learn about their "work-world"

2.13 "Space" Talk
Facilitate a team discussion to learn what type of "space" your employees need

2.14 Support Feedback
Receive feedback on your "supporting work" actions

90 Days

2.15 Mini-Assessment
Assess your "supporting work" progress

2.16 Bust-up the Roadblocks
Identify the obstacles and hurdles preventing you from improving your "supporting work" skills

2.17 External Practice
Identify "support" actions you will practice outside of work

2.18 Team Support Matrix
Identify how team members support each other

2.19 Supporting Actions Scorecard
Track how many times you perform "support" actions for your team members

Supporting Work
48 Hours

Prep Time **5 minutes**   *Action Time* **15 minutes**

2.1
Talk-it-Up!
Tell your manager, team, and peers you plan to improve your "supporting work" skills

Identify the individuals and/or groups who will be most impacted by a change in your "supporting work" skills and share your desire to improve your capabilities.

Step 1: In a team meeting, share your desire to improve your "supporting work" capabilities. Be sure to discuss the following:
- Explain "why" you have chosen to improve your "supporting work" skills
- Describe how an increase in performance will help you, the organization, and others
- Outline what you actions you plan to take to impact your capabilities

Step 2: Solicit the groups' help and feedback. Ask them to support your development by focusing on your "supporting work" actions from this point forward (not what you did in the past). Ask them to give you feedback on what you are doing well and what you need to improve.

Note: *Talk-it-Up!* is best done face-to-face, however, you can also *Talk-it-Up!* during a conference call or via email.

Supporting Work
48 Hours

Prep Time: **5 minutes** Action Time: **10 minutes**

Download electronic copy:
www.keeppeople.com/book/2.2.dot

2.2
Benefit Analysis
Determine whether improving your "supporting work" skills will be valuable for yourself and others

Complete a *Benefit Analysis* to determine whether improving your "supporting work" skills will be valuable for yourself and others.

Step 1: Identify the key individuals and/or groups who will be most impacted by a change in your "supporting work" skills. Record their names on the **Benefit Analysis Square** (page 77).

Step 2: For each individual or group, answer the following question:

"If you improve your "supporting work" capabilities, what benefits will be experienced by the individual or group?"

Identify two benefits for each individual or group, and record your responses on the *Benefit Analysis Square*.

Step 3: After completing the *Benefit Analysis Square*, determine whether the benefits of improving your "supporting work" capabilities outweigh the time and energy needed to improve your performance.

- If YES, move forward and take action to improve your "supporting work" capabilities
- If NO, select another manager capability to improve

Example

Your Employees
1. Each employee will receive the right "amount of space" from me to feel independent, supported, and successful
2. My employees will feel comfortable articulating the type of support they need from me.

Supporting Work
48 Hours

Prep Time **10 minutes** *Action Time* **10 minutes/employee**

2.3
Project Updates
Create a regularly schedule time slot for team members to give you updates on their work

Create and post dedicated time slots each week for team members to provide you updates on their current projects and deliverables.

Step 1: Share the purpose of the *Project Updates* with your team.

Step 2: Post your *Project Update* slots on your door, work space, or on an on-line calendar (e.g., Monday 2—4 p.m.).

Step 3: Team members should be able to schedule 10 minutes within the *Project Updates*, or be able to stop by your desk if you do not have a scheduled meeting with another team member.

Step 4: During the *Project Updates*, discuss the following with your employees:
- Recent developments with their projects or deliverables
- The status on each of their work projects
- Successes they have experienced
- Obstacles they have experienced
- Additional support they need from you to be successful

Step 5: Discuss the steps both you and the team member must take to ensure the team member can successfully achieve his or her goals and deliverables.

Note: Try to keep each *Project Update* to 10 minutes.

Supporting Work
48 Hours

Prep Time: 5 minutes Action Time: 10 minutes

Download electronic copy:
www.keeppeople.com/book/2.4.dot

2.4
Supporting Work Assessment
Evaluate the support you recently provided a team member

Evaluate the support you provided a team member in the last 45 days to identify actions you can take to improve the way you support your team members.

Step 1: Identify a time in the last 45 days when one of your team members received negative feedback from a client/customer, your manager, or others.

Step 2: Use the **Supporting Work Assessment** (page 78) to record the following:
1. Describe the situation
2. Identify how the employee would describe the support you gave him or her during this situation
3. Based on the circumstances and your view of the employee's perspective, what would you do differently in the future?

Step 3: Determine what actions you can take to improve the support you provide your team members.

Example

The Situation	Employee Perspective	Learning Actions
Our Director criticized Rick for handling a client poorly without finding out the facts first. When our Director confronted me with the situation, I agreed Rick must have done something wrong.	Rick would think I do not support him—he would think I am afraid to "stand up" to my Director.	I cannot jump to conclusions. I have a skilled and competent team who deserves the benefit of the doubt before being accused. In the future, I will explain to my Director that I am surprised by the negative comments, and that I want to find out the facts first—before I jump to conclusions.

Supporting Work
7 Days

Prep Time **5 minutes**

Action Time **60 minutes**

Download electronic copy:
www.keeppeople.com/book/2.5.dot

2.5
Two 4 U: Ideas for Improvement
Ask others for two ideas to improve your "supporting work" skills

Using the wisdom and experience from others, generate as many ideas as possible to improve your "supporting work" capabilities.

Step 1: Identify up to 5 people who have excellent "supporting work" skills.

Step 2: Ask each person the following question:

"I'm trying to improve my "supporting work" skills, do you have two ideas for how I can improve my capabilities?"

Step 3: Record each person's ideas on the **Two 4 U** (page 79) worksheet.

Step 4: Once you gathered ideas from each person, review the suggestions and circle the top three ideas you think will help the most.

Step 5: For your top three ideas, identify the next steps you will take to implement the idea.

Step 6: Thank the individuals who gave you the development ideas and share what actions you plan to take to improve your "supporting work" capabilities.

Supporting Work
7 Days

Prep Time 5 minutes   **Action Time** 15 minutes

Download electronic copy:
www.keeppeople.com/book/2.6.dot

2.6
Tracking Chart
Create a tracking chart to capture your "supporting work" progress

Each Friday capture what you actually completed during the week to improve your "supporting work" skills.

Step 1: Each Friday, identify and record the actions you took to improve your performance on the **Tracking Chart** (page 80).

Step 2: For each action, grade your performance based on how well you think you performed on the action, as well as considering feedback you may have received from others.

A = Excellent; B = Good; C = Average; D = Poor; F = Failing

Step 3: Based on your performance, identify one improvement action you will implement the following week.

Step 4: After completing the *Tracking Chat* ask yourself the following questions:
- Am I really taking actions to improve?
- Are my actions having the desired impact on my "supporting work" capabilities?

Example

Week	Supporting Work Actions	Grade
June 20	Created Project Education Update times	A
	Met with Greg to identify actions I can take to improve the support I give him	A
	Did not support Frank when he was under fire for his work on the BETA Project	F
Improvement Actions		
• Meet with Frank to identify actions I can take with others to show I support his work		

Supporting Work
7 Days

Prep Time **5 minutes** *Action Time* **10 minutes/ employee**

2.7
Assess My Support
Ask your employees to evaluate the support you provide them

Ask your team members to evaluate the level of support you provide to them.

Step 1: Send the following email to your team members:

I am currently working to improve my "supporting work" capabilities, and would like your help. Please take five minutes to evaluate the level of support I currently provide by answering the following questions:
1. *On a scale of 1 to 10 (1=I'm all alone; 10=You're always there when I need you)*
   - *How would you rate the current level of "support" you receive from me?*
   - *What level of "support" do you need from me to be successful in your job?*
2. *What specific actions can I take to make a difference in your "work-world"?*

Step 2: Follow-up with each team member (face-to-face or phone call) to discuss the level of "support" you give. During the follow-up discussion, identify actions you will take to improve the type of "support" you give the team member.

Supporting Work
7 Days

Prep Time **20 minutes** *Action Time* **5 minutes/employee**

Download electronic copy:
www.keeppeople.com/book/2.8.dot

2.8 Support Grid
Identify actions you will take in the future to increase the level of support you provide others

Review the support you've provided your team members in the last two weeks, and determine what additional actions you must take in the future to provide the support your employees need to be successful.

Step 1: Using the **Support Grid** (page 81) identify and record the following:

1. Actions you have taken in the last 2 weeks to "support" your employees and/or their work activities

2. A brief description of each team member's current work situation

3. Additional actions you must take in the future to improve the "support" you provide each team member

Step 2: Follow-up with your team members and share what actions you plan to take to ensure they receive the support they need to be successful.

Example

Team Member	Past Support Actions	Team Member Current Work Situation	Future Support Actions
Robert	Backed-off and let him "run" with the marketing plan	Would like to apply for the Marketing Director position	Show support for the marketing plan by promoting it to our Directors and have Robert present the plan at the next staff meeting

65

Supporting Work
7 Days

Prep Time
10 minutes

Action Time
45 minutes

2.9
Learning from Others
Ask a person who is really good at "supporting work" to give you feedback

Meet with a person who is great at "supporting work" to receive feedback on your "supporting work" actions, as well as receive ideas for actions you can take to improve your "supporting work" capabilities.

Step 1: Identify a person who you've worked with or worked for who is really good at "supporting" his or her employees.

Step 2: Ask this person to have lunch, coffee, or a conference call to discuss building your "supporting work" capabilities.

Step 3: During the discussion, be sure to ask the following questions:
- What lessons have you learned regarding "supporting" your team members?
- How have you handled _____ situation?
- What ideas do have to get really good at "supporting" team members' work?

Be sure to describe your current "supporting work" actions and ask the person to identify the strengths and weaknesses in your actions.

Supporting Work
30 Days

Prep Time **5 minutes** *Action Time* **45 minutes**

2.10
Team Discussion
Facilitate a team discussion to improve your "supporting work" skills

Solicit ideas from your team to improve your "supporting work" capabilities, and identify a way to receive immediate feedback as you implement your "supporting work" actions.

Step 1: In a team meeting share "why" you want to improve your "supporting work" skills, and share your thoughts about the importance of "supporting work" performance.

Step 2: Ask your team members to share how they think your "supporting work" capabilities impact the team and individual team members.

Step 3: Ask the team to brainstorm actions you can take to improve your "supporting work" skills.

Step 4: With the team, identify a way for team members to cue you when your actions are consistent, as well as inconsistent with the desired "supporting work" behaviors.

Try pick two hand gestures, statements, or signals to indicate when the new "supporting work" behaviors are happening and when they're not.

For example, team members may say *"Right on!"* when your behaviors are consistent, and *"Take a step back"* when your behaviors are inconsistent. Teams members may also use a hand gesture such as "thumbs-up" or "thumbs-down".

Supporting Work
30 Days

Prep Time **5 minutes** *Action Time* **2 hours**

Download electronic copy:
www.keeppeople.com/book/2.11.dot

2.11
Feedback for Me
Receive feedback on your "supporting work" actions

Solicit feedback on the actions you have taken to improve your "supporting work" capabilities.

Step 1: Identify up to 5 people who can give you feedback on your "supporting work" actions, and send them the following email:

> *I have chosen to take action to improve my "supporting work" skills and would like some help from you. In the next 30 to 45 days, I'd like to follow-up with you to receive feedback on my "supporting work" performance. When we talk, I will ask you the following questions:*
> 1. *What "supporting work" actions have you seen me perform?*
> 2. *What impact have my actions created for individuals, the team, and/or the organization?*
> 3. *What improvement ideas do you have for me?*
>
> *Thank you for your help. I look forward to speaking with you soon.*

Step 2: Identify a follow-up date when you will ask each person for feedback. Record the date on the **Feedback for Me** (page 82) worksheet.

Step 3: At the time of your follow-up dates, schedule a 15 minute discussion with each person to receive feedback on your "supporting work" actions.

Step 4: After receiving feedback, record the feedback on the *Feedback for Me* worksheet. Be sure to thank each person for his or her time and willingness to provide you feedback on your "supporting work" actions.

Step 5: Based on the feedback you received, think about the following:
- What "supporting work" actions do I need to do more of?
- What actions do I need to do less of?
- What additional actions should I integrate into my "supporting work" improvement plan?

Supporting Work
30 Days

Prep Time
5 minutes

Action Time
20 minutes/ employee

2.12
Education Session
Spend time with each of your employees to learn about their "work-world"

Meet with your team members to learn about their "work-world", and identify what you can do to help them be successful.

Step 1: Schedule a 15 to 20 minute discussion with your team members.

Step 2: During the discussion, ask the following questions to learn about their "work-world":

- Who really helps and hinders your progress?

- What changes need to happen in your "work-world" to increase your effectiveness? (e.g., the technology you use, the information you receive)

- What are the best and worst parts of your "work-world"?

- What are your recent achievements and successes?

- What do you need from me to be successful?

During the *Education Session*, be curious, and actively listen to your employee's words and messages "behind the word". You should walk away with a sense of what it's like to spend a day "in their shoes".

Step 3: Based on your discussion, identify the actions you can take to help the team member be successful in his or her role.

Supporting Work
30 Days

Prep Time 5 minutes   *Action Time* 45 minutes

2.13
"Space" Talk
Facilitate a team discussion to learn what type of "space" your employees need

Meet with your team to discuss the amount of "space" they need to successfully deliver their goals and objectives.

Step 1: In a team meeting, explain why you have chosen to improve your "supporting work" capabilities.

Step 2: Ask the team to discuss the following:

What is the right amount of "space" (elbow room, autonomy, and decision authority) you need to work?

Step 3: Have your team members discuss a situation when they:
1. Didn't have enough "space" to do their work
2. Had the right balance of freedom and autonomy

Step 4: Based on the team discussion, identify and share the "supporting work" actions you will take to improve the type of "support" you provide your team.

Supporting Work **30 Days**	*Prep Time* **5 minutes**	*Action Time* **60 minutes**

Download electronic copy:
www.keeppeople.com/book/2.14.dot

2.14
Support Feedback
Receive feedback on your "supporting work" actions

Facilitate a feedback session with your team to understand what type of support you provide your team members.

Step 1: In a team meeting, explain why you have chosen to improve your "supporting work" capabilities, and share your thoughts regarding the importance of "supporting work".

Step 2: Ask your team to discuss and summarize the statements on the **Support Feedback** (page 83) worksheet.

Step 3: LEAVE THE ROOM. Your team should discuss the questions without you. This process will provide the most honest feedback to help you improve your "supporting work" capabilities.

Step 4: After you leave the room, each team member should spend 10 minutes thinking about his or her own responses to the *Support Feedback* questions.

Step 5: The group should then summarize the individual responses; adding, deleting, or modifying responses to create a concise group summary.

Step 6: After summarizing the responses, the group should invite you back into the room to review their *Support Feedback* summary.

Step 7: Based on the team discussion, identify and share the actions you will take in the future to improve your "supporting work" capabilities. Thank the team for their honest feedback.

Supporting Work
90 Days

Prep Time
10 minutes

Action Time
30 minutes

Download electronic copy:
www.keeppeople.com/book/2.15.pdf

2.15
Mini-Assessment
Assess your "supporting work" performance progress

Determine if your "supporting work" actions are perceived as more effective.

45 Days Before the Mini-Assessment:
Step 1: Identify the individuals and/or groups who will be most impacted by a change in your "supporting work" capabilities and share your desire to improve your "supporting work" skills.

Step 2: Explain "why" you have chosen to improve your "supporting work" capabilities. Describe how an increase in performance will help you, the organization, and others.

Step 3: Solicit their help and feedback. Ask the individuals to support your development by observing your actions for 45 days. Tell them at the end of the 45 days you will give them a *Mini-Assessment* to evaluate your "supporting work" actions.

The Mini-Assessment:
Step 4: After 45 days, give a copy of the **Mini-Assessment** (page 84) to the individuals you asked to observe your behaviors—ask them to complete the *Mini-Assessment* honestly.

Step 5: Request the individuals return the assessment to you when they are finished.

Step 6: Summarize your results for each statement. Where do you have strengths and weaknesses?

Step 7: Identify actions you will take based on your *Mini-Assessment* results.

Step 8: Share these actions with the individuals who gave you feedback and thank them for their help.

Supporting Work
90 Days

Prep Time: 5 minutes
Action Time: 15 minutes

Download electronic copy:
www.keeppeople.com/book/2.16.dot

2.16
Bust-up the Roadblocks
Identify the obstacles and hurdles preventing you from improving your "supporting work" skills

Identify why you may not be taking action to improve your "supporting work" skills, and/or determine why the actions you have taken are not having the desired impact.

Step 1: Record your current and planned "supporting work" actions on the **Bust-up the Roadblocks** (page 85) worksheet.

Step 2: Review each action and determine if a "roadblock" or obstacle is preventing you from implementing a planned action or preventing a current action from creating its desired impact.

Step 3: Based on the "roadblock", identify "bust-up" actions you can take to eliminate or manage the roadblock.

Example

Current and Planned "Supporting Work" Actions	"Roadblock" or Obstacle	"Bust-up" Action
I plan to perform an Education Session with each team member in the next 6 weeks.	I don't have the time to meet with all my team members for an Education Session within the next 6 weeks.	In the next 6 weeks I will meet with team members who are at risk of disengaging from their work or leaving the team. Once I meet with these team members, I'll schedule additional Education Sessions.

Supporting Work
90 Days

Prep Time
10 minutes

Action Time
TBD

2.17
External Practice
Identify "support" actions you will practice outside of work

Use outside organizations to practice building your "supporting work" capabilities.

Step 1: Think about the different groups and individuals you are involved in outside your work (your family, school boards, church, professional organizations, etc.).

Step 2: Choose one of these individuals or groups to practice "support actions" with.

Step 3: Use the following questions to help you identify two actions you will take to practice "supporting" others:
- What can you do in the next meeting or interaction to increase the level of "support" you provide the individual or group?

- What can you do to learn from other individuals you are good at "supporting" others?

Step 4: Implement your identified actions.

Supporting Work
90 Days

Prep Time **10 minutes** *Action Time* **90 minutes**

2.18
Team Support Matrix
Identify how team members support each other

Facilitate a discussion with your team members to identify how each individual "supports" others members on the team.

Step 1: Recreate the *Team Support Matrix* below on a flip chart or dry erase board.

Step 2: Record each team member's name on the matrix (be sure to include yourself on the matrix).

Step 3: In a team meeting, ask your team members to identify how they "support" each other, and record the actions on the *Team Support Matrix*.

Step 4: Ask a team member to recreate the matrix and provide a copy to each team member).

Step 5: Discuss the *Team Support Matrix* periodically during a team meeting, conference call, or off-site meeting to reinforce how each team member provides critical "support" to others.

Example

		SUPPORTEE *(What we receive from others)*		
		Ann	**Tom**	**"You"**
SUPPORTER *(What we do for others)*	**Ann**		Ann provides weekly project reports to Tom	Ann ensures all project invoices are processed within 2 days
	Tom	Tom is a Project Management resource for Ann		Tom manages all Associate Project Managers
	"You"	You are the point of contact for all obstacles/issues facing the BETA Project	You provide feedback to Tom regarding his coaching skills	

Supporting Work
90 Days

Prep Time
5 minutes

Action Time
15 minutes/week

Download electronic copy:
www.keeppeople.com/book/2.19.dot

2.19
Supporting Actions Scorecard
Track how many times you perform "support" actions for your team members

Within a 30-day time period, see how many times you can perform the actions on the *Supporting Actions Scorecard* for your team members.

Step 1: Each Friday, identify and record the interactions you've had with your team members over the last week on the **Supporting Actions Scorecard** (page 86).

Step 2: For each interaction, mark the "support actions" you performed, and record who received the "support".

Step 3: Review the scorecard and answer the following questions:

- Are you balancing your "support" across team members?
- Are you relying on a few ways to "support" them?
- As you look back at your actions, are you <u>really</u> showing "support" for your employees?

Step 4: Identify what actions you must take to increase the level of "support" you give your team members.

Supporting Work

2.2
Benefit Analysis Square

For each individual or group, answer the following question:

"If you improve your "supporting work" capabilities, what benefits will be experienced by the individual or group?"

Identify two benefits for each individual or group, and record your responses below.

Determine whether the benefits of improving your "supporting work" capabilities outweigh the time and energy needed to improve your performance.

- If YES, move forward and take action to improve your "supporting work" capabilities
- If NO, select another manager capability to improve

Yourself	Your Manager	Your Employees
1.	1.	1.
2.	2.	2.

Your Peers & Co-Workers	Benefits	Key Customers & Clients
1.		1.
2.		2.

Your Significant Other/Family	Other _____	Other _____
1.	1.	1.
2.	2.	2.

Supporting Work

2.4
Supporting Work Assessment

Identify a time in the last 45 days when one of your team members received negative feedback from a client/customer, your manager, or others.

Record the following below:
- Describe the situation
- Identify how the employee would describe the support you gave him or her during this situation
- Based on the circumstances and your view of the employee's perspective, what would you do differently in the future?

Determine what actions you can take to improve the support you provide your team members.

The Situation	Employee Perspective	Learning Actions

Supporting Work

2.5
Two 4 U

Identify up to 5 people who have excellent "supporting work" skills and ask each person the following question:

"I'm trying to improve my "supporting work" skills, do you have two ideas for how I can improve my capabilities?"

Record each person's ideas below. Once you gathered ideas from each person, review the suggestions and circle the top three ideas you think will help the most.

For your top three ideas, identify the next steps you will take to implement the idea.

Individual	Idea #1	Idea #2	Next Steps

Supporting Work

2.6
Tracking Chart

Each Friday, identify and record the actions you took to improve your performance. For each action, grade your performance based on how well you think you performed on the action, as well as considering feedback you may have received from others.

A = Excellent; B = Good; C = Average; D = Poor; F = Failing

Based on your performance, identify one improvement action you will implement the following week.

Week	Supporting Work Actions	Grade
Improvement Action:		
Improvement Action:		
Improvement Action:		

Supporting Work

2.8
Support Grid
Identify and record the following:

1. Actions you have taken in the last 2 weeks to "support" your employees and/or their work activities
2. A brief description of each team member's current work situation
3. Additional actions you must take in the future to improve the "support" you provide each team member

Team Member	Past Support Actions	Team Member Current Work Situation	Future Support Actions

Supporting Work

2.11
Feedback for Me

Identify up to 5 people who can give you feedback on your "supporting work" actions. Determine when you will follow-up with each person and record the date below.

After receiving feedback, record the feedback from each person.

Based on the feedback you received, think about the following:
- What "supporting work" actions do I need to do more of?
- What actions do I need to do less of?
- What additional actions should I integrate into my "supporting work" improvement plan?

Name	Follow-Up Date	Feedback		
		What "supporting work" actions have you seen me perform?	*What impact have my actions created for individuals, the team, and/or the organization?*	*What improvement ideas do you have for me?*

Supporting Work

2.14
Support Feedback

Review the following "supporting work" statements. Based on your manager's actions, jot down your responses to each question. Share your responses with the team to create an overall team response for each question.

"Supporting Work" Statements	Response
My best "stand-up and support me" experience was...	
My worst "stand-up and support me" experience was...	
My manager should have "backed off" and allowed team members to work on...	
My manager is guilty of "micromanaging" the following...	
My manager needs to learn more about _____ work...	
My manager is not well informed around the area of...	
People outside our group don't know how much my manager "supports"...	

Supporting Work

2.15
Mini-Assessment

A little over a month ago I began improving my "supporting work" capabilities. Please help me gauge my performance by taking 5 minutes to answer a few questions. Please return the assessment with the enclosed envelope.

Thank you for your feedback!

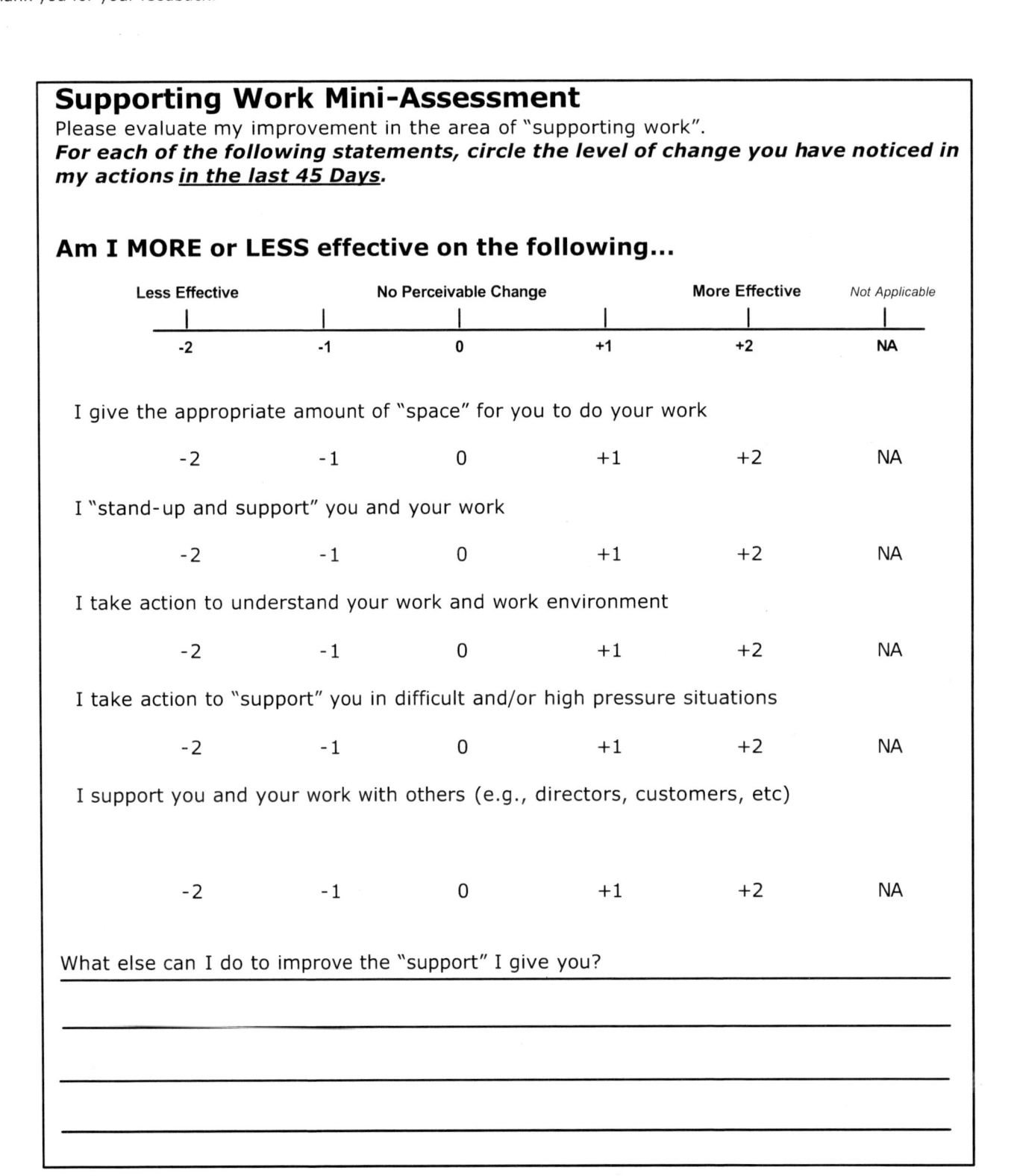

Supporting Work Mini-Assessment

Please evaluate my improvement in the area of "supporting work".

For each of the following statements, circle the level of change you have noticed in my actions <u>in the last 45 Days</u>.

Am I MORE or LESS effective on the following...

Less Effective	No Perceivable Change	More Effective	Not Applicable
-2 -1	0	+1 +2	NA

I give the appropriate amount of "space" for you to do your work

-2   -1   0   +1   +2   NA

I "stand-up and support" you and your work

-2   -1   0   +1   +2   NA

I take action to understand your work and work environment

-2   -1   0   +1   +2   NA

I take action to "support" you in difficult and/or high pressure situations

-2   -1   0   +1   +2   NA

I support you and your work with others (e.g., directors, customers, etc)

-2   -1   0   +1   +2   NA

What else can I do to improve the "support" I give you?
_____
_____
_____
_____

Supporting Work

2.16
Bust-up the Roadblocks

Record your current and planned "supporting work" actions below. Review each action and determine if a "roadblock" or obstacle is preventing you from implementing a planned action or preventing a current action from creating its desired impact. Based on the "roadblock", identify "bust-up" actions you can take to eliminate or manage the roadblock.

Current and Planned "Supporting Work" Actions	"Roadblock" or Obstacle	"Bust-up" Action

Supporting Work

2.19
Supporting Actions Scorecard

Within a 30-day time period see how many times you can perform the *Manager Support Actions*. Identify and record the interactions you've had with your employees over the last week. For each interaction, mark the "support actions" you performed and record who received the "support".

	Employee Interaction			
	Date	*Date*	*Date*	*Date*
Manager Support Actions	**Team Member**	**Team Member**	**Team Member**	**Team Member**
Aked questions about an employee's work				
Gave the "right amount" of space				
Supported employee's actions with a client				
Fought for Resources				
Said "No" to a Request				
Presented position or "stance" to upper management				
Outlined rationale for action or decision				
Asked what level of "support" the employee needs from me				
Helped Problem Solve				

Providing Feedback

Deliver frequent and specific feedback to help employees improve their performance

Providing Feedback

48 Hours

3.1 Talk-it-Up!
Tell your manager, team, and peers you plan to improve your "feedback" skills

3.2 Benefit Analysis
Determine whether improving your "feedback" skills will be valuable for yourself and others

3.3 Feedback Guide
Use the Feedback Guide to improve the effectiveness of your feedback

3.4 Feedback Counter
Keep track of the number of times you provide feedback

7 Days

3.5 Two 4 U: Ideas for Improvement
Ask others for two ideas to improve your "feedback" skills

3.6 Tracking Chart
Create a tracking chart to capture your "feedback" progress

3.7 Assess My Feedback
Ask your employees to evaluate the feedback you provide them

3.8 Giving Feedback Audit
Evaluate the feedback you've given your team members

30 Days

3.9 Team Discussion
Facilitate a team discussion to improve your "feedback" skills

3.10 Feedback for Me
Receive feedback on your "feedback" actions

3.11 Feedback Network
Increase the amount of feedback your team members receive from others

3.12 Feedback Actions
Keep track of the feedback actions you take with your team members

3.13 Employee Feedback Session
Perform a feedback session with each of your employees

90 Days

3.14 Mini-Assessment
Assess your "feedback" progress

3.15 Bust-up the Roadblocks
Identify the obstacles and hurdles preventing you from improving your "feedback" skills

3.16 Feedback Mentor
Use a mentor to help you improve your feedback skills

3.17 25 Ways to Reinforce Desired Results
Increase the actions you take to reinforce your team members' performance

3.18 Team Feedback Session
Facilitate a feedback session with your team

Providing Feedback
48 Hours

Prep Time **5 minutes** *Action Time* **15 minutes**

3.1
Talk-it-Up!
Tell your manager, team, and peers you plan to improve your feedback skills

Identify the individuals and/or groups who will be most impacted by a change in your feedback skills and share your desire to improve your capabilities.

Step 1: In a team meeting, share your desire to improve your feedback capabilities. Be sure to discuss the following:
- Explain "why" you have chosen to improve your feedback skills
- Describe how an increase in performance will help you, the organization, and others
- Outline what you actions you plan to take to impact your capabilities

Step 2: Solicit the groups' help and feedback. Ask them to support your development by focusing on your feedback actions from this point forward (not what you did in the past). Ask them to give you feedback on what you are doing well and what you need to improve.

Note: *Talk-it-Up!* is best done face-to-face, however, you can also *Talk-it-Up!* during a conference call or via email.

Providing Feedback
48 Hours

Prep Time **5 minutes** *Action Time* **10 minutes**

Download electronic copy:
www.keeppeople.com/book/3.2.dot

3.2
Benefit Analysis
Determine whether improving your feedback skills will be valuable for yourself and others

Complete a *Benefit Analysis* to determine whether improving your feedback skills will be valuable for yourself and others.

Step 1: Identify the key individuals and/or groups who will be most impacted by a change in your feedback skills. Record their names on the **Benefit Analysis Square** (page 110).

Step 2: For each individual or group, answer the following question:

"If you improve your feedback capabilities, what benefits will be experienced by the individual or group?"

Identify two benefits for each individual or group, and record your responses on the *Benefit Analysis Square*.

Step 3: After completing the *Benefit Analysis Square*, determine whether the benefits of improving your feedback capabilities outweigh the time and energy needed to improve your performance.

- If YES, move forward and take action to improve your feedback capabilities
- If NO, select another manager capability to improve

Example

Your Employees
1. My employees will always know their current level of performance
2. My employees will receive performance feedback in comfortable and appropriate settings.

Providing Feedback
48 Hours

Prep Time **5 minutes**   *Action Time* **15 minutes**

Download electronic copy:
www.keeppeople.com/book/3.3.pdf

3.3
Feedback Guide
Use the Feedback Guide to improve the effectiveness of your feedback

Use the *Feedback Guide* when giving feedback to your team members to ensure your feedback positively impacts individual and team results.

Step 1: Review the **Feedback Guide** (page 111) before giving feedback to your team member.

Step 2: Before you give feedback to your team member, review the roles of the Giver and Receiver in the DIRECT Feedback Loop.

Step 3: When giving feedback, follow the steps outlined in the DIRECT Feedback Loop.

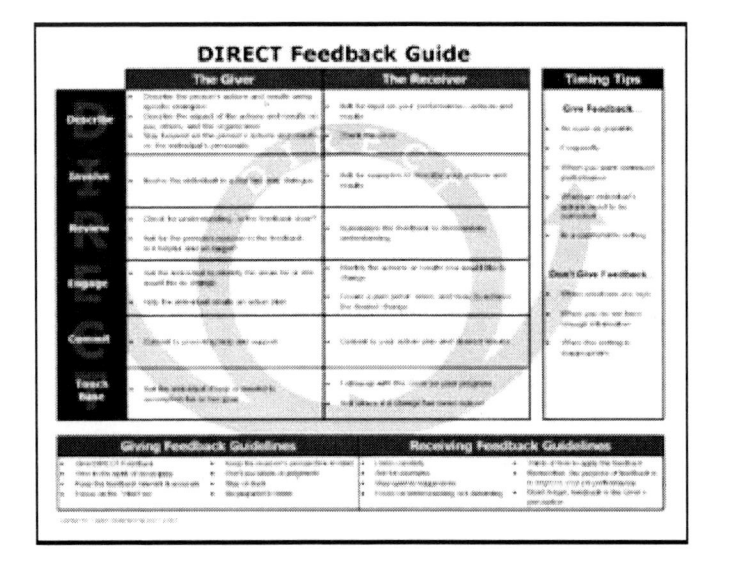

Providing Feedback
48 Hours

Prep Time **5 minutes** *Action Time* **15 minutes**

3.4
Feedback Counter
Keep track of the number of times you provide feedback

Integrate a quick and easy counting method into your work day to keep track of the number of times you provide positive feedback to your team members.

Step 1: Select three to five small objects you can keep in your pocket throughout the day (e.g., paperclips, pennies, or beads).

Step 2: At the beginning of each day, place the objects in your right pocket.

Step 3: Each time you provide feedback to one of your team members, move one of the objects from your right pocket into your left pocket.

- Your goal should be to have an empty right pocket, and a full left pocket, at the end of the day.

If you find it easy to consistently move all the objects to your left pocket, challenge yourself and increase the number of objects you start with.

Providing Feedback
7 Days

Prep Time
5 minutes

Action Time
60 minutes

Download electronic copy:
www.keeppeople.com/book/3.5.dot

3.5
Two 4 U: Ideas for Improvement
Ask others for two ideas to improve your feedback skills

Using the wisdom and experience from others, generate as many ideas as possible to improve your feedback capabilities.

Step 1: Identify up to 5 people who have excellent feedback skills.

Step 2: Ask each person the following question:

"I'm trying to improve my feedback skills, do you have two ideas for how I can improve my capabilities?"

Step 3: Record each person's ideas on the **Two 4 U** worksheet (page 112).

Step 4: Once you gathered ideas from each person, review the suggestions and circle the top three ideas you think will help the most.

Step 5: For your top three ideas, identify the next steps you will take to implement the idea.

Step 6: Thank the individuals who gave you the development ideas and share what actions you plan to take to improve your feedback capabilities.

Providing Feedback
7 Days

Prep Time
5 minutes

Action Time
10 minutes

Download electronic copy:
www.keeppeople.com/book/3.6.dot

3.6
Tracking Chart
Create a tracking chart to capture your feedback progress

Each Friday capture what you actually completed during the week to improve your feedback skills.

Step 1: Each Friday, identify and record the actions you took to improve your performance on the **Tracking Chart** (page 113).

Step 2: For each action, grade your performance based on how well you think you performed on the action, as well as considering feedback you may have received from others.

A = Excellent; B = Good; C = Average; D = Poor; F = Failing

Step 3: Based on your performance, identify one improvement action you will implement the following week.

Step 4: After completing the *Tracking Chat* ask yourself the following questions:
- Am I really taking actions to improve?
- Are my actions having the desired impact on my feedback capabilities?

Example

Week	Feedback Actions	Grade
October 13	Used the Feedback Guide when I gave feedback to Kevin about his presentation	B
	Gave Eric corrective feedback at his desk—two co-workers overheard me talking	F
	Stopped myself from giving corrective feedback to Kate at her desk—we met in my office instead	A
Improvement Actions • Schedule One-to-One's with all employees to give performance feedback • Apologize to Eric for giving him corrective feedback at his desk		

Providing Feedback
7 Days

Prep Time **5 minutes**

Action Time **10 minutes/employee**

3.7
Assess My Feedback
Ask your employees to evaluate the feedback you provide them

Ask your team members to evaluate the type of feedback you provide to them.

Step 1: Send the following email to your team members:

> *I am currently working to improve my "feedback" capabilities, and would like your help.*
> *Please take five minutes to evaluate the type of feedback I currently provide by answering the following questions:*
> 1. On a scale of 1 to 10 (1=I never know where I stand; 10=I always know what I'm doing well and where I should improve)
>   - How would you rate the current feedback you receive from me?
> 2. Please choose the statement which best describes the feedback you receive from me:
>   - Specific, Clear, and Timely **OR** Generic, Vague, and Too Late
>   - A _real_ two-way dialogue **OR** a monologue (I'm talking _at_ you)
>   - Focused on the "most critical" actions **OR** Focused on everything "under-the-sun"
> 3. What area do you want me to provide _more_ feedback on to help you succeed?

Step 2: Follow-up with each team member (face-to-face or phone call) to discuss the type of feedback you give. During the follow-up discussion, identify actions you will take to improve the feedback you give the team member.

Providing Feedback
7 Days

Prep Time **5 minutes**   *Action Time* **15 minutes**

Download electronic copy:
www.keeppeople.com/book/3.8.pdf

3.8
Giving Feedback Audit
Evaluate the feedback you've given your team members

Think about the last time you gave performance feedback to each of your team members and rate your performance for each feedback session.

Step 1: Write the names of your team members on the **Feedback Audit** worksheet (page 114).

Step 2: For each team member, think about your most recent feedback session with the team member and perform the following:

1. Review each *Feedback Criteria* and answer Yes or No for each question based on your performance during the feedback session

2. Circle your response to each question in the team member's column

Step 3: Review your performance for each team member, and identify what you will do differently with the team member next time you give him or her performance feedback. Record these actions on the *Feedback Audit* worksheet.

Example

	Feedback Criteria	Team Member *Chris*	Team Member *Doug*	Team Member *Anne*	Team Member *Ryan*
1	Did you give this employee feedback **as soon as possible**?	(Yes) No	(Yes) No	Yes (No)	Yes (No)
2	Was the setting **comfortable and appropriate** for the employee?	(Yes) No	Yes (No)	Yes (No)	(Yes) No

Providing Feedback
30 Days

Prep Time **5 minutes** *Action Time* **45 minutes**

3.9
Team Discussion
Facilitate a team discussion to improve your feedback skills

Solicit ideas from your team to improve your feedback capabilities, and identify a way to receive immediate feedback as you implement your feedback actions.

Step 1: In a team meeting share "why" you want to improve your feedback skills, and share your thoughts about the importance of feedback.

Step 2: Ask your team members to share how they think your feedback capabilities impact the team and individual team members.

Step 3: Ask the team to brainstorm actions you can take to improve your feedback skills.

Step 4: With the team, identify a way for team members to cue you when your actions are consistent, as well as inconsistent with the desired feedback behaviors.

Try pick two hand gestures, statements, or signals to indicate when the new feedback behaviors are happening and when they're not.

For example, team members may say *"Right on!"* when your behaviors are consistent, and *"Take a step back"* when your behaviors are inconsistent. Teams members may also use a hand gesture such as "thumbs-up" or "thumbs-down".

Providing Feedback
30 Days

Prep Time 5 minutes

Action Time 2 hours

Download electronic copy:
www.keeppeople.com/book/3.10.dot

3.10
Feedback for Me
Receive feedback on your "feedback" actions

Solicit feedback on the actions you have taken to improve your feedback capabilities.

Step 1: Identify up to 5 people who can give you feedback on your feedback actions, and send them the following email:

> *I have chosen to take action to improve my feedback skills and would like some help from you. In the next 30 to 45 days, I'd like to follow-up with you to receive feedback on my "feedback" performance. When we talk, I will ask you the following questions:*
> 1. *What feedback actions have you seen me perform?*
> 2. *What impact have my actions created for individuals, the team, and/or the organization?*
> 3. *What improvement ideas do you have for me?*
>
> *Thank you for your help. I look forward to speaking with you soon.*

Step 2: Identify a follow-up date when you will ask each person for feedback. Record the date on the **Feedback for Me** worksheet (page 115).

Step 3: At the time of your follow-up dates, schedule a 15 minute discussion with each person to receive feedback on your feedback actions.

Step 4: After receiving feedback, record the feedback on the *Feedback for Me* worksheet. Be sure to thank each person for his or her time and willingness to provide you feedback on your feedback actions.

Step 5: Based on the feedback you received, think about the following:
- What feedback actions do I need to do more of?
- What actions do I need to do less of?
- What additional actions should I integrate into my feedback improvement plan?

Providing Feedback
30 Days

Prep Time
5 minutes

Action Time
15 minutes/ employees

Download electronic copy:
www.keeppeople.com/book/3.11.dot

3.11
Feedback Network
Increase the amount of feedback your team members receive from others

With your team members, create a Feedback Network of individuals who will be able to provide performance feedback to the team member.

Step 1: With each team member, identify the skills and capabilities, projects, or individual objectives, the team member would like feedback on.

Step 2: Based on the desired feedback, identify two individuals who can provide feedback to the team member.

Step 3: Record the names of the individuals on the **Feedback Network** worksheet (page 116), and identify the specific skill or capability, project, or objective the individual can provide feedback on.

Step 4: Team members should solicit feedback when needed, and schedule dedicated time to receive direct feedback from the individuals within his or her Feedback Network.

Providing Feedback
30 Days

Prep Time **25 minutes** *Action Time* **60 minutes**

Download electronic copy:
www.keeppeople.com/book/3.12.pdf
www.keeppeople.com/book/3.12a.pdf

3.12
Feedback Actions
Keep track of the feedback actions you take with your team members

Use the Feedback Actions to ensure you provide the feedback your team members need to deliver high performing results.

Step 1: Print the **Feedback Cards** (page 117) for each team member. Cut out the cards, and give all four cards to each team member.

Step 2: Ask your team members to pay attention to your feedback actions, and return each card once they "experience" you performing the feedback action on the card.

Step 3: When you receive a card from a team member, check-off the card in the team member's column on the **Feedback Action Chart** (page 118), recording the date you received the card.

Step 4: As you begin to receive the cards back from your team members, review the *Feedback Action Chart* and think about the following questions:
- Is there one feedback action you do more of or less of?
- Are you more effective at providing feedback to some team members versus others?
- Who do you need to improve your feedback actions with?

See if you can get all four cards back from each team member within 30 days.

Providing Feedback
30 Days

Prep Time
10 minutes/ employee

Action Time
30 minutes/ employee

3.13
Employee Feedback Session
Perform a feedback session with each of your employees

Schedule a feedback session with your team members to provide performance feedback.

Step 1: Schedule a one-to-one feedback session with each team member.

Step 2: Before you meet with a team member, outline the following:
- What are the team member's current projects and deliverables?
- What is the team member's current level of performance?
- What actions must the team member continue doing to achieve success?
- What actions must the team member discontinue to achieve success?

Step 3: Meet with the team member to provide the feedback outlined in Step 2.

Step 4: Provide the opportunity for the team member to ask questions, get clarification, and provide additional performance information.

Step 5: Outline the actions both you and the team member must take to ensure the team member is successfully able to deliver his or her goals and objectives.

Providing Feedback
90 Days

Prep Time **10 minutes** *Action Time* **30 minutes**

Download electronic copy:
www.keeppeople.com/book/3.14.pdf

3.14
Mini-Assessment
Assess your feedback performance progress

Determine if your feedback actions are perceived as more effective.

45 Days Before the Mini-Assessment:
Step 1: Identify the individuals and/or groups who will be most impacted by a change in your feedback capabilities and share your desire to improve your feedback skills.

Step 2: Explain "why" you have chosen to improve your feedback capabilities. Describe how an increase in performance will help you, the organization, and others.

Step 3: Solicit their help and feedback. Ask the individuals to support your development by observing your actions for 45 days. Tell them at the end of the 45 days you will give them a *Mini-Assessment* to evaluate your feedback actions.

The Mini-Assessment:
Step 4: After 45 days, give a copy of the **Mini-Assessment** (page 119) to the individuals you asked to observe your behaviors—ask them to complete the *Mini-Assessment* honestly.

Step 5: Request the individuals return the assessment to you when they are finished.

Step 6: Summarize your results for each statement. Where do you have strengths and weaknesses?

Step 7: Identify actions you will take based on your *Mini-Assessment* results.

Step 8: Share these actions with the individuals who gave you feedback and thank them for their help.

Providing Feedback
90 Days

Prep Time **5 minutes**   *Action Time* **15 minutes**

Download electronic copy:
www.keeppeople.com/book/3.15.dot

3.15
Bust-up the Roadblocks
Identify the obstacles and hurdles preventing you from improving your feedback skills

Identify why you may not be taking action to improve your feedback skills, and/or determine why the actions you have taken are not having the desired impact.

Step 1: Record your current and planned feedback actions on the **Bust-up the Roadblocks** worksheet (page 120).

Step 2: Review each action and determine if a "roadblock" or obstacle is preventing you from implementing a planned action or preventing a current action from creating its desired impact.

Step 3: Based on the "roadblock", identify "bust-up" actions you can take to eliminate or manage the roadblock.

Example

Current and Planned Feedback Actions	"Roadblock" or Obstacle	"Bust-up" Action
I plan to perform a Feedback Session with each team member in the next 6 weeks.	I don't have the time to meet with all my team members for a Feedback Session within the next 6 weeks.	In the next 6 weeks I will meet with team members who are at risk for achieving their deliverables. Once I meet with these team members, I'll schedule additional Feedback Sessions.

Providing Feedback
90 Days

Prep Time **15 minutes** *Action Time* **TBD**

3.16
Feedback Mentor
Use a mentor to help you improve your feedback skills

Identify a person who is great at giving feedback and is willing to help you build your feedback skills.

Step 1: Identify a person who you are currently working with or have worked with in the past who is excellent at giving feedback to others.

Step 2: Ask the individual if he or she would be willing to help you over the next 60 days to build your feedback skills.

Step 3: As situations occur in which you must provide performance feedback to others, implement at least one of the following actions:

1. **Before** you give any feedback, plan your feedback and present it to your mentor. Ask for additional methods or ideas for presenting the feedback.

2. **After** giving feedback, share the experience with your mentor. Identify the strengths and weaknesses of your feedback, and outline future actions.

Note: Working with a mentor will help you identify the areas you need to improve, while gaining valuable insight and wisdom from a feedback expert.

Providing Feedback
90 Days

Prep Time **10 minutes**

Action Time **TBD**

Download electronic copy:
www.keeppeople.com/book/3.17.dot

3.17
25 Ways to Reinforce Desired Results
Increase the actions you take to reinforce your team members' performance

Select specific actions you will implement for your team members to reinforce desired performance.

Step 1: Review the reinforcement actions on the **25 Ways to Reinforce Desired Performance** worksheet (page 121). Circle or highlight the actions you will implement with your team members.

Step 2: As you complete an action, record the team member's name and date you performed the action.

Step 3: Each week, tally the number of actions you took to reinforce performance that week.

Note: You can keep a record of the reinforcement actions you implement for each team member (copy the worksheet for each team member), or you can keep one record for the entire team.

Providing Feedback
90 Days

Prep Time
10 minutes

Action Time
90 minutes

3.18
Team Feedback Session
Facilitate a feedback session with your team

Facilitate a team discussion to outline what team members must do (day-to-day, week-to-week) to deliver "high performing results".

Step 1: In a team meeting, discuss the team's performance by using the questions below to create a clear picture of the team's current performance.
- What results has the team achieved?
- What results were NOT delivered?
- If an outsider observed the team for a week, what actions would this person see?
- On a scale of 1 to 10 (1 = "we're the worst we can be"; 10 = "we're the best we can be"), how would you rate the team's current performance?

Step 2: Based on the team's current performance, identify the actions all team members must take in the following areas to deliver high performing results:

Start: What actions do team members need to start doing?
(e.g., *Provide weekly project status updates*)

Stop: What actions do team members need to stop doing?
(e.g., *Arriving for and starting meetings late*)

Continue: What actions do team members need to continue doing?
(e.g., *Recognizing each other's good work*)

Step 3: Review the profile periodically (in meetings, conference calls, etc.) to highlight the teams' consistency with the actions needed to deliver high performing results.

Providing Feedback

3.2
Benefit Analysis Square

For each individual or group, answer the following question:

"If you improve your "feedback" capabilities, what benefits will be experienced by the individual or group?"

Identify two benefits for each individual or group, and record your responses below.

Determine whether the benefits of improving your "feedback" capabilities outweigh the time and energy needed to improve your performance.

- If YES, move forward and take action to improve your "feedback" capabilities
- If NO, select another manager capability to improve

Yourself	Your Manager	Your Employees
1.	1.	1.
2.	2.	2.

Your Peers & Co-Workers	**Benefits**	Key Customers & Clients
1.		1.
2.		2.

Your Significant Other/Family	Other _____	Other _____
1.	1.	1.
2.	2.	2.

DIRECT Feedback Guide

Timing Tips

Give Feedback…
- As soon as possible
- Frequently
- When you want continued performance
- When an individual's actions need to be corrected
- In a comfortable setting

Don't Give Feedback…
- When emotions are high
- When you do not have enough information
- When the setting is inappropriate

	The Giver	The Receiver
D – Describe	• Describe the person's actions and results using specific examples. • Describe the impact of the actions and results on you, others, and the organization • Stay focused on the person's actions and results vs. the individual's personality.	• Ask for input on your performance—actions and results. • Thank the Giver.
I – Involve	• Involve the individual in a real two-way dialogue.	• Ask for examples to describe your actions and results.
R – Review	• Check for understanding…is the feedback clear? • Ask for the person's reaction to the feedback. Is it helpful and on target?	• Summarize the feedback to demonstrate understanding.
E – Engage	• Ask the individual to identify the areas he or she would like to change. • Help the individual create an action plan.	• Identify the actions or results you would like to change. • Create a plan (what, when, and how) to achieve the desired change.
C – Commit	• Commit to providing help and support.	• Commit to your action plan and desired results.
T – Touch Base	• Ask the individual if help is needed to accomplish his or her goal.	• Follow-up with the Giver on your progress. • Ask others if a change has been noticed.

Giving Feedback Guidelines

- Give DIRECT Feedback
- Give in the spirit of developing
- Keep the feedback relevant & accurate
- Focus on the "Vital Few"
- Keep the receiver's perspective in mind
- Don't use labels or judgments
- Stay on track
- Be prepared to listen

Receiving Feedback Guidelines

- Listen carefully
- Ask for examples
- Stay open to suggestions
- Focus on understanding, not defending
- Think of how to apply the feedback
- Remember, the purpose of feedback is to improve your job performance
- Don't forget, feedback is the Giver's perception

Center for Talent Retention © 2001-2005

Providing Feedback

3.5
Two 4 U

Identify up to 5 people who have excellent "feedback" skills and ask each person the following question:

"I'm trying to improve my "feedback" skills, do you have two ideas for how I can improve my capabilities?"

Record each person's ideas below. Once you gathered ideas from each person, review the suggestions and circle the top three ideas you think will help the most.

For your top three ideas, identify the next steps you will take to implement the idea.

Individual	Idea #1	Idea #2	Next Steps

Providing Feedback

3.6
Tracking Chart

Each Friday, identify and record the actions you took to improve your performance. For each action, grade your performance based on how well you think you performed on the action, as well as considering feedback you may have received from others.

A = Excellent; B = Good; C = Average; D = Poor; F = Failing

Based on your performance, identify one improvement action you will implement the following week.

Week	Feedback Actions	Grade

Improvement Action:

Improvement Action:

Improvement Action:

Providing Feedback

3.8
Giving Feedback Audit

Write the names of your team members below. For each team member, think about your most recent feedback session with the team member and perform the following:
1. Review each *Feedback Criteria* and answer Yes or No for each question based on your performance during the feedback session
2. Circle your response to each question in the team member's column

Review your performance for each team member, and identify what you will do differently with the team member next time you give him or her performance feedback. Record these actions below.

	Feedback Criteria	Team Member	Team Member	Team Member	Team Member	Team Member	Team Member
1	Did you give this employee feedback **as soon as possible**?	Yes　No	Yes　No	Yes　No	Yes　No	Yes　No	Yes　No
2	Was the setting **comfortable and appropriate** for the employee?	Yes　No	Yes　No	Yes　No	Yes　No	Yes　No	Yes　No
3	Did you give the feedback when **your emotions were too high**?	Yes　No	Yes　No	Yes　No	Yes　No	Yes　No	Yes　No
4	Did you use **labels or judgments**?	Yes　No	Yes　No	Yes　No	Yes　No	Yes　No	Yes　No
5	Did you use **specific examples** to describe the impact of the employee's behavior?	Yes　No	Yes　No	Yes　No	Yes　No	Yes　No	Yes　No
6	Did you stay **focused on behaviors and results** versus focusing on the employee?	Yes　No	Yes　No	Yes　No	Yes　No	Yes　No	Yes　No
7	Did you stay on track and **focus on the most important information**?	Yes　No	Yes　No	Yes　No	Yes　No	Yes　No	Yes　No
8	Did you really listen to the employee and **create a two-way dialogue**?	Yes　No	Yes　No	Yes　No	Yes　No	Yes　No	Yes　No

Future Actions	
Team Member	**Actions**

Providing Feedback

3.10
Feedback for Me

Identify up to 5 people who can give you feedback on your "feedback" actions. Determine when you will follow-up with each person and record the date below.

After receiving feedback, record the feedback from each person.

Based on the feedback you received, think about the following:
- What "feedback" actions do I need to do more of?
- What actions do I need to do less of?
- What additional actions should I integrate into my "feedback" improvement plan?

Name	Follow-Up Date	\multicolumn{3}{c}{Feedback}
		What "feedback" actions have you seen me perform?	*What impact have my actions created for individuals, the team, and/or the organization?*	*What improvement ideas do you have for me?*

Center for Talent Retention © 2000-2005

Providing Feedback

3.11
Feedback Network

Record the names of the individuals who can provide feedback to the team member, as well as the skill or capability, project, or objective they can provide feedback on.

	Feedback Resource #1
Name	
Skill or Capability, Project, or Objective	
	Feedback Resource #2
Name	
Skill or Capability, Project, or Objective	

Providing Feedback

3.12
Feedback Cards
Cut out the cards below.

Pay attention to the feedback you receive from your manager and team members. When you "experience" one of the actions below, return the card to your manager.

---

(1) I received feedback from my manager on something I am doing well.

(2) I received feedback from a team member on something I am doing well.

(3) I received feedback from my manager or team members on something I need to change.

(4) My manager asked me for feedback.

Providing Feedback

3.12
Feedback Action Chart

When you receive the Feedback Cards from your team members, check-off the card in the team member's column and record the date you received the card.

As you begin to receive the cards back from your team members think about the following:
- Is there one feedback action you do more of or less of?
- Are you more effective at providing feedback to some team members versus others?
- Who do you need to improve your feedback actions with?

Feedback Card	Team Member Name	Team Member Name	Team Member Name	Team Member Name	Team Member Name
(1) I received feedback from my manager on something I am doing well.	☐ _____ Date received	☐ _____ Date received	☐ _____ Date received	☐ _____ Date received	☐ _____ Date received
(2) I received feedback from a team member on something I am doing well.	☐ _____ Date received	☐ _____ Date received	☐ _____ Date received	☐ _____ Date received	☐ _____ Date received
(3) I received feedback from my manager or team members on something I need to change.	☐ _____ Date received	☐ _____ Date received	☐ _____ Date received	☐ _____ Date received	☐ _____ Date received
(4) My manager asked me for feedback.	☐ _____ Date received	☐ _____ Date received	☐ _____ Date received	☐ _____ Date received	☐ _____ Date received

Providing Feedback

3.14
Mini-Assessment

A little over a month ago I began improving my "feedback" capabilities. Please help me gauge my performance by taking 5 minutes to answer a few questions. Please return the assessment with the enclosed envelope.

Thank you for your feedback!

Feedback Mini-Assessment

Please evaluate my improvement in the area of "providing feedback".

For each of the following statements, circle the level of change you have noticed in my actions <u>in the last 45 Days</u>.

Am I MORE or LESS effective on the following...

Less Effective		No Perceivable Change		More Effective	Not Applicable
-2	-1	0	+1	+2	NA

I give you helpful and effective performance feedback

    -2   -1   0   +1   +2   NA

You receive feedback on a consistent basis

    -2   -1   0   +1   +2   NA

I give you feedback in comfortable and appropriate settings

    -2   -1   0   +1   +2   NA

You have a number of people to receive feedback from

    -2   -1   0   +1   +2   NA

My feedback reflects a "real" picture of your performance

    -2   -1   0   +1   +2   NA

What else can I do to improve the "feedback" I give you?

_____

_____

_____

_____

Providing Feedback

3.15
Bust-up the Roadblocks

Record your current and planned feedback actions below. Review each action and determine if a "roadblock" or obstacle is preventing you from implementing a planned action or preventing a current action from creating its desired impact. Based on the "roadblock", identify "bust-up" actions you can take to eliminate or manage the roadblock.

Current and Planned Feedback Actions	"Roadblock" or Obstacle	"Bust-up" Action

Providing Feedback

3.17
25 Ways to Reinforce Desired Performance

Circle or highlight the actions you will implement with your team. As you complete an action, record the team member's name and date you completed the action.

#	25 Reinforcement Actions	Team Member	Date
1	Send a note to an employee's significant other describing how much you value and appreciate the employee's contributions		
2	Leave a surprise (e.g., candy bar, balloon, trophy, certificate of achievement) on an employee's chair—be sure to leave a note of appreciation		
3	Send a group distribution voicemail to your manager and the team regarding an employee's performance		
4	Ask a key customer or client to share with an employee how he or she is helping them be successful		
5	Send a group email describing how an employee's performance is helping the organization		
6	Discuss the positive impact of an employee's actions on a conference call		
7	At the end of a meeting or conference call describe what you thought went well during the meeting/call		
8	Send an employee to represent you or the organization in an important meeting		
9	Ask an employee to teach the rest of the team an area he or she is performing well in		
10	Present an accomplishment achieved by an employee to your team		
11	Tell an employee you are confident in his or her capability in _____ area		
12	Personally congratulate an employee for a job well done by shaking his or her hand		
13	Ask your manager or the director of your workgroup to call an employee to recognize a job well done		
14	Ask an employee to mentor another employee in an area he or she is very knowledgeable in		
15	Create an opportunity for an employee to work on a "pet project" as a reward for a great achievement		
16	Thank an employee for a task/job which is "taken for granted"		
17	When introducing a peer, new team member, or co-worker to an employee, tell the person about one of the employee's successes		
18	Tell an employee about one action he or she is really good at and describe how the action impacts the team		
19	When you hear a positive remark about an employee, share it with that employee as soon as possible		
20	Leave a post-it note on the employee's desk saying, "Thanks for being part of the team—We would not be able to accomplish _____ without you."		
21	Ask an employee to present a project he or she completed to <u>your</u> manager or the sponsor of the project		
22	In a team meeting, highlight an employee's behavior and say, "That is exactly what we need everyone to do to be successful."		
23	Share an employee's success with your peers and direct reports—be sure to tell the employee you did this		
24	In a team meeting, describe the team's top three strengths and outline how they positively impact the organization		
25	At the end of the day, tell an employee what he or she did well that day—describe how it impacts you, the team, and the organization		

Center for Talent Retention © 2000-2005

Establishing Credibility

Role model words and actions that build credibility with others

Establishing Credibility

48 Hours

4.1 Talk-it-Up!
Tell your manager, team, and peers you plan to improve your "credibility" with others

4.2 Benefit Analysis
Determine whether improving your "credibility" will be valuable for yourself and others

4.3 Credibility Self-Assessment
Identify the actions you need to do "more of" and "less of" to improve your credibility

4.4 Current Commitments
Learn how to plan your actions to meet your personal commitments

7 Days

4.5 Two 4 U: Ideas for Improvement
Ask others for two ideas to improve your "credibility"

4.6 Tracking Chart
Create a tracking chart to capture your "credibility" progress

4.7 Straight Talk
Inform your team about an issue they received partial, mixed, or no information

4.8 Credibility Zappers
Determine which of your actions have the greatest impact on your credibility

30 Days

4.9 Team Discussion
Facilitate a team discussion to improve your "credibility"

4.10 Feedback for Me
Receive feedback on your "credibility" actions

4.11 Tough Issue Talk
Build 5 to 10 minutes in team meetings to discuss difficult issues

4.12 Credibility in Action
Determine how well your actions and behaviors match your work priorities

4.13 In-the-Know
Help your employees gain an understanding of team and organization issues

90 Days

4.14 Mini-Assessment
Assess your "credibility" progress

4.15 Bust-up the Roadblocks
Identify the obstacles and hurdles preventing you from improving your "credibility"

4.16 Walk-the-Talk Audit
During meetings, determine if the team's actions were consistent with the team values, goals, and priorities

4.17 Team Feedback
Ask your team to answer "credibility" questions and present their responses back to you

4.18 Commitment Log
Keep track of the commitments you make and how well you keep them

Establishing Credibility
48 Hours

Prep Time **5 minutes**   *Action Time* **15 minutes**

4.1
Talk-it-Up!
Tell your manager, team, and peers you plan to improve your credibility

Identify the individuals and/or groups who will be most impacted by a change in your credibility and share your desire to improve your capabilities.

Step 1: In a team meeting, share your desire to improve your credibility. Be sure to discuss the following:
- Explain "why" you have chosen to improve your credibility
- Describe how an increase in performance will help you, the organization, and others
- Outline what you actions you plan to take to impact your capabilities

Step 2: Solicit the groups' help and feedback. Ask them to support your development by focusing on your credibility from this point forward (not what you did in the past). Ask them to give you feedback on what you are doing well and what you need to improve.

Note: *Talk-it-Up!* is best done face-to-face, however, you can also *Talk-it-Up!* during a conference call or via email.

Establishing Credibility
48 Hours

Prep Time 5 minutes *Action Time* 10 minutes

Download electronic copy:
www.keeppeople.com/book/4.2.dot

4.2
Benefit Analysis
Determine whether improving your credibility will be valuable for yourself and others

Complete a *Benefit Analysis* to determine whether improving your credibility will be valuable for yourself and others.

Step 1: Identify the key individuals and/or groups who will be most impacted by a change in your credibility. Record their names on the **Benefit Analysis Square** (page 144).

Step 2: For each individual or group, answer the following question:

> *"If you improve your credibility, what benefits will be experienced by the individual or group?"*

Identify two benefits for each individual or group, and record your responses on the *Benefit Analysis Square*.

Step 3: After completing the *Benefit Analysis Square*, determine whether the benefits of improving your credibility outweigh the time and energy needed to improve your performance.

- If YES, move forward and take action to improve your credibility
- If NO, select another manager capability to improve

Example

Your Employees
1. My team members can take action based on complete and accurate information.
2. My team members will know "what I say" is "what I do".

Establishing Credibility
48 Hours

Prep Time: 15 minutes
Action Time: TBD

Download electronic copy:
www.keeppeople.com/book/4.3.dot

4.3
Credibility Self-Assessment
Identify the actions you need to do "more of" and "less of" to improve your credibility

Determine the actions you must continue and discontinue to build your credibility.

Step 1: Review the statements on the **Credibility Self-Assessment** worksheet (page 145), and think about your personal actions and behaviors.

Step 2: For each statement, determine what you need to do "more of" and "less of" to positively impact your credibility. Think about what really happens most of the time, not what you would like to have happen, or what happens some of the time. If we were a "fly on-the-wall" what would we see?

Step 3: Record your responses on the worksheet.

Step 4: Periodically review your self-assessment to determine if you were able to increase the actions you need to do "more of", and reduce or eliminate the actions you need to do "less of".

Note: *We judge ourselves mostly by our intentions—however, others judge us mostly by our actions.*

Example

Credibility Statement	I need to do MORE of...	I need to do LESS of...
Withholding Information	Share information about Project BETA as soon as I receive it.	Keep "negative" information to myself for fear of upsetting my team members

Establishing Credibility
48 Hours

Prep Time: 30 minutes
Action Time: TBD

Download electronic copy:
www.keeppeople.com/book/4.4.dot

4.4
Current Commitments
Learn how to plan your actions to meet your personal commitments

Plan your actions to meet your commitments and avoid procrastination.

Step 1: Identify your current commitments to the individuals and/or groups on the **Current Commitments** chart (page 146).

Step 2: For each individual or group, rank your commitments from LEAST DESIRABLE (#1) to MOST DESIREABLE (#4).

> **LEAST DESIREABLE** = An action or commitment you like the LEAST or don't want to do
>
> **MOST DESIREABLE** = An action or commitment you like the MOST and look forward to doing

Step 3: Record your "ranked" commitments on the *Current Commitments* chart based on their desirability. Be sure to make your least desired commitment #1.

Step 4: Each time you complete a commitment, cross it off on the chart.

Note: Completing your commitments from "least desirable" to "most desirable" helps avoid procrastination, while rewarding you for completing a commitment. Each time you finish a commitment you will be moving to one you like better!

Example

Least Desirable ──────────────────────────▶ Most Desirable

Individual/Group	Commitment #1	Commitment #2	Commitment #3	Commitment #4
My Manager				
Karen	Outline budget for the next 6 months	Provide corrective feedback to Josh	Facilitate a team brainstorming session for Project Y	N/A

129

Establishing Credibility
7 Days

Prep Time
5 minutes

Action Time
60 minutes

Download electronic copy:
www.keeppeople.com/book/4.5.dot

4.5
Two 4 U: Ideas for Improvement
Ask others for two ideas to improve your credibility

Using the wisdom and experience from others, generate as many ideas as possible to improve your credibility.

Step 1: Identify up to 5 people who have excellent credibility.

Step 2: Ask each person the following question:

"I'm trying to improve my credibility skills, do you have two ideas for how I can improve my capabilities?"

Step 3: Record each person's ideas on the **Two 4 U** worksheet (page 147).

Step 4: Once you gathered ideas from each person, review the suggestions and circle the top three ideas you think will help the most.

Step 5: For your top three ideas, identify the next steps you will take to implement the idea.

Step 6: Thank the individuals who gave you the development ideas and share what actions you plan to take to improve your credibility.

Establishing Credibility
7 Days

Prep Time
5 minutes

Action Time
10 minutes

Download electronic copy:
www.keeppeople.com/book/4.6.dot

4.6
Tracking Chart
Create a tracking chart to capture your credibility progress

Each Friday capture what you actually completed during the week to improve your credibility.

Step 1: Each Friday, identify and record the actions you took to improve your performance on the **Tracking Chart** (page 148).

Step 2: For each action, grade your performance based on how well you think you performed on the action, as well as considering feedback you may have received from others.

A = Excellent; B = Good; C = Average; D = Poor; F = Failing

Step 3: Based on your performance, identify one improvement action you will implement the following week.

Step 4: After completing the *Tracking Chat* ask yourself the following questions:
- Am I really taking actions to improve?
- Are my actions having the desired impact on my credibility?

Example

Week	Credibility Actions	Grade
January 17	I told Frank I would not be able to complete the report three days before it was due	B
	Held a team meeting to discuss the rumors about the cancellation of our project—I shared what I knew	A
	Committed to Greg to deliver a project plan I knew I would have trouble completing in time	F
Improvement Actions		
• Discuss my schedule with Greg to determine if the project plan due date can be changed or if someone else should take the lead		

Establishing Credibility
7 Days

Prep Time
20 minutes

Action Time
30 minutes

4.7
Straight Talk
Inform your team about an issue they received partial, mixed, or no information

Select an area in which your team received partial, mixed, or no information, and create a *Straight Talk Story* to "set the record" straight.

Step 1: Identify an area your team received partial, mixed, or no information on.

Step 2: Using the statements below, write a *Straight Talk Story* for your team members.

> *Once upon a time there was _____ situation, and most people thought _____. As everyone discussed the history surrounding _____ and _____ recent events, they would always end up thinking _____. What everyone doesn't know is _____ and _____. You see, the future of our organization requires _____ and _____. Without these capabilities, we will not achieve _____ results. The _____ situation impacts us in _____ and _____ ways. For our team and the organization to be successful, people need to do more of _____ and less of _____. What I will be doing to help make this happen is _____, and what I need from you to make this happen is _____. The End.*

Step 3: Read your *Straight Talk Story* in a team meeting. Encourage your team to ask questions and get clarification until they have a solid understand of the actual situation.

Note: If needed, add more statements to help "set the record straight" or increase the level of "in-the-know".

Establishing Credibility
7 Days

Prep Time
15 minutes

Action Time
TBD

Download electronic copy:
www.keeppeople.com/book/4.8.pdf

4.8
Credibility Zappers
Determine which of your actions have the greatest impact on your credibility

Do you "zap" your credibility with others? Use the *Credibility Zappers* to determine which "zappers" impact your credibility.

Step 1: Review the "zappers" on the **Credibility Zapper** worksheet (page 149).

Step 2: For each credibility "zapper", think about your past behaviors and determine which rating best describes your past actions and behaviors. Record your score.

Step 3: Total your credibility "zapper" scores, and review your rating.

Step 4: Based on your rating, identify what actions you can take to reduce the number of "zappers" impacting your credibility.

Example

Credibility Zapper	Never +10	Rarely +5	Sometimes -5	Often -10	Score
I am untruthful	○	○	●	○	-5
I exaggerate or embellish situations	○	●	○	○	+5
I restrict or hold back information from others	○	○	○	●	-10

Establishing Credibility
30 Days

Prep Time **5 minutes**

Action Time **45 minutes**

4.9
Team Discussion
Facilitate a team discussion to improve your credibility

Solicit ideas from your team to improve your credibility, and identify a way to receive immediate feedback as you implement your credibility.

Step 1: In a team meeting share "why" you want to improve your credibility, and share your thoughts about the importance of credibility.

Step 2: Ask your team members to share how they think your credibility impact the team and individual team members.

Step 3: Ask the team to brainstorm actions you can take to improve your credibility.

Step 4: With the team, identify a way for team members to cue you when your actions are consistent, as well as inconsistent with the desired credibility.

Try pick two hand gestures, statements, or signals to indicate when the new credibility behaviors are happening and when they're not.

For example, team members may say *"Right on!"* when your behaviors are consistent, and *"Take a step back"* when your behaviors are inconsistent. Teams members may also use a hand gesture such as "thumbs-up" or "thumbs-down".

Establishing Credibility
30 Days

Prep Time
5 minutes

Action Time
2 hours

Download electronic copy:
www.keeppeople.com/book/4.10.dot

4.10
Feedback for Me
Receive feedback on your credibility

Solicit feedback on the actions you have taken to improve your credibility.

Step 1: Identify up to 5 people who can give you feedback on your credibility, and send them the following email:

> *I have chosen to take action to improve my credibility and would like some help from you. In the next 30 to 45 days, I'd like to follow-up with you to receive feedback on my "credibility" performance. When we talk, I will ask you the following questions:*
> 1. *What credibility actions have you seen me perform?*
> 2. *What impact have my actions created for individuals, the team, and/or the organization?*
> 3. *What improvement ideas do you have for me?*
>
> *Thank you for your help. I look forward to speaking with you soon.*

Step 2: Identify a follow-up date when you will ask each person for feedback. Record the date on the **Feedback for Me** worksheet (page 150).

Step 3: At the time of your follow-up dates, schedule a 15 minute discussion with each person to receive feedback on your credibility.

Step 4: After receiving feedback, record the feedback on the *Feedback for Me* worksheet. Be sure to thank each person for his or her time and willingness to provide you feedback on your credibility.

Step 5: Based on the feedback you received, think about the following:
- What credibility actions do I need to do more of?
- What actions do I need to do less of?
- What additional actions should I integrate into my credibility improvement plan?

Establishing Credibility
30 Days

Prep Time **5 minutes**

Action Time 30 minutes/meeting

4.11
Tough Issue Talk
Build 5 to 10 minutes in team meetings to discuss difficult issues

In team meetings, discuss difficult team or organization issues with your team members.

Step 1: Set aside 5 to 10 minutes in your team meetings to discuss a difficult or imperative team or organization issue (e.g., poor team performance, inappropriate behaviors, employee changes, changes in senior leadership, etc.).

Step 2: Select the first issue you will discuss with your team.

Step 3: In a team meeting perform the following:
1. Describe the issue
2. Present the information you know
3. Share your personal thoughts
4. Discuss the impact on individuals and the team

Step 4: Ask your team members to share additional information and their own thoughts.

Step 5: When the discussion is finished, ask the team to select an issue for the next meeting.

Establishing Credibility
30 Days

Prep Time 10 minutes *Action Time* 15 minutes/week

Download electronic copy:
www.keeppeople.com/book/4.12.dot

4.12
Credibility in Action
Determine how well your actions and behaviors match your work priorities

Determine how well your work priorities (what you say) match your actions and behaviors (what you do).

Step 1: Identify your work priorities and record them on the **Credibility in Action** worksheet (page 151).

Step 2: Each week, review the action categories and record the actions you took that week for each category.

Step 3: Based on your current actions, determine if your actions and behaviors support or contradict your work priorities.

Step 3: Identify future actions you can take to increase the consistency between "what you say" and "what you do".

Example

Action Category	My Current Actions	Future Actions
My Schedule *How I spend my time*	I accept meetings knowing I may have to cancel them due to previous commitments.	I will not schedule a meeting unless I have my calendar with me.

Establishing Credibility
30 Days

Prep Time
10 minutes

Action Time
15 minutes/ meeting

4.13
In-the-Know
Help your employees gain an understanding of team and organization issues

Create the opportunity for team members to receive additional information or clarification on team or organization issues.

Step 1: In a team meeting, describe the *In-the-Know* process, and share how you would like to provide the opportunity for team members to receive information and clarity regarding team and organization issues.

Step 2: When team members want to know more about a team or organization issue, ask your team members email you the question/issue, or drop it off in your mailbox.

Step 3: Prepare to address the identified issue in an upcoming meeting or conference call. When discussing the issue, be sure to:

- Describe the issue
- Share what you know about the issue
- Outline the benefits and drawbacks of the situation
- Clarify your role and the team's role in the situation
- Discuss what you and the team can expect to happen in the future

Establishing Credibility
90 Days

Prep Time **10 minutes**   *Action Time* **30 minutes**

Download electronic copy:
www.keeppeople.com/book/4.14.pdf

4.14
Mini-Assessment
Assess your credibility performance progress

Determine if your credibility actions are perceived as more effective.

45 Days Before the Mini-Assessment:
Step 1: Identify the individuals and/or groups who will be most impacted by a change in your credibility and share your desire to improve your credibility.

Step 2: Explain "why" you have chosen to improve your credibility. Describe how an increase in performance will help you, the organization, and others.

Step 3: Solicit their help and feedback. Ask the individuals to support your development by observing your actions for 45 days. Tell them at the end of the 45 days you will give them a *Mini-Assessment* to evaluate your credibility.

The Mini-Assessment:
Step 4: After 45 days, give a copy of the **Mini-Assessment** (page 152) to the individuals you asked to observe your behaviors—ask them to complete the *Mini-Assessment* honestly.

Step 5: Request the individuals return the assessment to you when they are finished.

Step 6: Summarize your results for each statement. Where do you have strengths and weaknesses?

Step 7: Identify actions you will take based on your *Mini-Assessment* results.

Step 8: Share these actions with the individuals who gave you feedback and thank them for their help.

Establishing Credibility
90 Days

Prep Time: **5 minutes** Action Time: **10 minutes**

Download electronic copy:
www.keeppeople.com/book/4.15.dot

4.15
Bust-up the Roadblocks
Identify the obstacles and hurdles preventing you from improving your credibility

Identify why you may not be taking action to improve your credibility, and/or determine why the actions you have taken are not having the desired impact.

Step 1: Record your current and planned credibility actions on the **Bust-up the Roadblocks** worksheet (page 153).

Step 2: Review each action and determine if a "roadblock" or obstacle is preventing you from implementing a planned action or preventing a current action from creating its desired impact.

Step 3: Based on the "roadblock", identify "bust-up" actions you can take to eliminate or manage the roadblock.

Example

Current and Planned Credibility Actions	"Roadblock" or Obstacle	"Bust-up" Action
I plan to receive feedback on my credibility actions over the last 8 weeks.	I haven't asked for the feedback for fear of receiving negative feedback from my team members.	If I don't ask for feedback, I won't know how I'm doing, and therefore I won't be able to improve. I will hand out the Mini-Assessment in our next team meeting. I'll ask my team members to fill it out anonymously and return it to my mailbox.

Establishing Credibility
90 Days

Prep Time
5 minutes

Action Time
5 minutes/ meeting

4.16
Walk-the-Talk Audit
During meetings, determine if the team's actions were consistent with the team values, goals, and priorities

In each team meeting, perform a quick audit to determine if the team's actions were consistent with the team values, goals, and priorities.

Step 1: For the next 60 to 90 days, make the last agenda item of any team meeting or conference call the *Walk-the-Talk Audit*.

Step 2: At the end of each meeting, as a team, spend 5 minutes discussing the following question:

> **Were our actions and decisions during this meeting consistent or inconsistent with our team values, priorities, and/or goals?**
>
> (e.g., We say customer service is important, but all of our time was focused on how the new changes would impact team members versus our customers.)

Note: If the team's values, priorities, and goals are unclear, spend time discussing them before starting the *Walk-the-Talk Audits*.

Establishing Credibility
90 Days

Prep Time **10 minutes** *Action Time* **90 minutes**

Download electronic copy:
www.keeppeople.com/book/4.17.dot

4.17
Team Feedback
Ask your team to answer "credibility" questions and present their responses back to you

Facilitate a feedback session with your team to understand how you build credibility with others.

Step 1: In a team meeting, explain why you have chosen to improve your "credibility" and share your thoughts regarding the importance of "credibility".

Step 2: Ask your team to discuss and summarize the statements on the **Team Feedback** worksheet (page 154).

Step 3: LEAVE THE ROOM. Your team should discuss the questions without you. This process will provide the most honest feedback to help you improve your "credibility".

Step 4: After you leave the room, each team member should spend 10 minutes thinking about his or her own responses to the *Team Feedback* questions.

Step 5: The group should then summarize the individual responses; adding, deleting, or modifying responses to create a concise group summary.

Step 6: After summarizing the responses, the group should invite you back into the room to review their *Team Feedback* summary.

Step 7: Based on the team discussion, identify and share the actions you will take in the future to improve your "credibility". Thank the team for their honest feedback.

Establishing Credibility
90 Days

Prep Time **10 minutes** *Action Time* **TBD**

Download electronic copy:
www.keeppeople.com/book/4.18.dot

4.18
Commitment Log
Keep track of the commitments you make and how well you keep them

Determine how well you meet your commitments using the *Commitment Log*.

Step 1: Each time you make a commitment, record it on the **Commitment Log** (page 155). For example, you make a commitment to perform a task, follow-up with a phone call, or find out a piece of information. Be sure to identify who the action is for and when it is due.

Step 2: For each action, rate the level of completion you achieved.

Step 3: Each week, review your *Commitment Log* and think about the following:

- Are there certain actions you tend to avoid?
- Do you have trouble meeting your commitments for certain individuals?

Step 4: Determine what actions can you take to improve your ability to meet future commitments.

Note: If you can't meet a commitment, talk to the person or group before the due date. Explain why you will not be able to meet the date, and set a new one.

Don't penalize yourself for commitments in which circumstances eliminate your need to complete it—simply cross the action off your list.

Establishing Credibility

4.2
Benefit Analysis Square

For each individual or group, answer the following question:

"If you improve your "credibility", what benefits will be experienced by the individual or group?"

Identify two benefits for each individual or group, and record your responses below.

Determine whether the benefits of improving your "credibility" outweigh the time and energy needed to improve your performance.

- If YES, move forward and take action to improve your "credibility"
- If NO, select another manager capability to improve

Yourself	Your Manager	Your Employees
1.	1.	1.
2.	2.	2.

Your Peers & Co-Workers	**Benefits**	Key Customers & Clients
1.		1.
2.		2.

Your Significant Other/Family	Other _____	Other _____
1.	1.	1.
2.	2.	2.

Establishing Credibility

4.3
Credibility Self-Assessment

Review the statements below, and think about your personal actions and behaviors. For each statement, determine what you need to do "more of" and "less of" to positively impact your credibility. Think about what really happens most of the time, not what you would like to have happen, or what happens some of the time. If we were a "fly on-the-wall" what would we see?

Credibility Statements	I need to do MORE of...	I need to do LESS of...
Saying one thing and doing another		
Being Untruthful		
Missing Deadlines		
Withholding Information		
Sending Mixed Signals or Information		

Establishing Credibility

4.4
Current Commitments

Identify your current commitments to the individuals and/or groups below. For each individual or group, rank your commitments from LEAST DESIRABLE (#1) to MOST DESIREABLE (#4).

LEAST DESIREABLE = An action or commitment you like the LEAST or don't want to do

MOST DESIREABLE = An action or commitment you like the MOST and look forward to doing

Record your "ranked" commitments on the *Current Commitments* chart based on their desirability. Be sure to make your least desired commitment #1. Each time you complete a commitment, cross it off on the chart.

Least Desirable ⟶ Most Desirable

Individual/Group	Commitment #1	Commitment #2	Commitment #3	Commitment #4
My Manager				
Team Member				
Team Member				
Peers				
My Significant Other				
My Family				
Myself				
Other				

Establishing Credibility

4.5
Two 4 U

Identify up to 5 people who have excellent "credibility" and ask each person the following question:

"I'm trying to improve my" credibility", do you have two ideas for how I can improve my credibility?"

Record each person's ideas below. Once you gathered ideas from each person, review the suggestions and circle the top three ideas you think will help the most.

For your top three ideas, identify the next steps you will take to implement the idea.

Individual	Idea #1	Idea #2	Next Steps

Establishing Credibility

4.6
Tracking Chart

Each Friday, identify and record the actions you took to improve your performance. For each action, grade your performance based on how well you think you performed on the action, as well as considering feedback you may have received from others.

A = Excellent; B = Good; C = Average; D = Poor; F = Failing

Based on your performance, identify one improvement action you will implement the following week.

Week	Credibility Actions	Grade

Improvement Action:

Week	Credibility Actions	Grade

Improvement Action:

Week	Credibility Actions	Grade

Improvement Action:

Establishing Credibility

4.8
Credibility Zappers

For each credibility "zapper", think about your past behaviors and determine which rating best describes your past actions and behaviors. Record your score.

Total your credibility "zapper" scores, and review your rating.

Credibility Zapper	Never +10	Rarely +5	Sometimes -5	Often -10	Score
I am untruthful	○	○	○	○	
I exaggerate or embellish situations	○	○	○	○	
I restrict or hold back information from others	○	○	○	○	
I tell "secrets"	○	○	○	○	
I selectively share information	○	○	○	○	
I don't deliver what I commit to	○	○	○	○	
I avoid certain subjects	○	○	○	○	
I say one thing and do another	○	○	○	○	
I don't act how I want others to act	○	○	○	○	
I tell one person one thing and others something else	○	○	○	○	
				TOTAL	

Rating		
-100 to -50 points	**POOR:**	Your credibility with others is terrible—you must take immediate action to improve your credibility
-49 to 0 points	**FAIR:**	Your credibility is questionable—identify actions you will take to improve your credibility with others
+1 to +60 points	**GOOD:**	You are on your way to establishing good credibility with others—continue to monitor your actions
+61 to +100 points	**EXCELLENT:**	You are building great credibility with others—keep up the good work

Establishing Credibility

4.10
Feedback for Me

Identify up to 5 people who can give you feedback on your "credibility" actions. Determine when you will follow-up with each person and record the date below.

After receiving feedback, record the feedback from each person.

Based on the feedback you received, think about the following:
- What "credibility" actions do I need to do more of?
- What actions do I need to do less of?
- What additional actions should I integrate into my "credibility" improvement plan?

Name	Follow-Up Date	Feedback		
		What "credibility" actions have you seen me perform?	*What impact have my actions created for individuals, the team, and/or the organization?*	*What improvement ideas do you have for me?*

Establishing Credibility

4.12
Credibility in Action

Identify your work priorities and record them below. Each week, review the action categories and record the actions you took that week for each category. Based on your current actions, determine if your actions and behaviors support or contradict your work priorities. Identify future actions you can take to increase the consistency between "what you say" and "what you do".

My Work Priorities — What I say...
1.
2.
3.
4.
5.

Action Category	What I do... My Current Actions	Future Actions
My Schedule *How I spend my time*		
My Words *What I talk about*		
Commitments to Others *What I do*		
Rewarding and Recognizing Others *What I reinforce*		

Establishing Credibility

4.14
Mini-Assessment

A little over a month ago I began improving my "credibility". Please help me gauge my performance by taking 5 minutes to answer a few questions. Please return the assessment with the enclosed envelope.

Thank you for your feedback!

Credibility Mini-Assessment

Please evaluate my improvement in the area of "establishing credibility".

For each of the following statements, circle the level of change you have noticed in my actions <u>in the last 45 Days</u>.

Am I MORE or LESS effective on the following...

Less Effective		No Perceivable Change		More Effective	Not Applicable
-2	-1	0	+1	+2	NA

I meet my commitments to you

    -2   -1   0   +1   +2   NA

I do not withhold information from you or the team

    -2   -1   0   +1   +2   NA

My actions are consistent with my words

    -2   -1   0   +1   +2   NA

I am truthful

    -2   -1   0   +1   +2   NA

I share difficult information with you and the team

    -2   -1   0   +1   +2   NA

What else can I do to improve my "credibility" with you?

_____

_____

_____

_____

Establishing Credibility

4.15
Bust-up the Roadblocks

Record your current and planned "credibility" actions below. Review each action and determine if a "roadblock" or obstacle is preventing you from implementing a planned action or preventing a current action from creating its desired impact. Based on the "roadblock", identify "bust-up" actions you can take to eliminate or manage the roadblock.

Current and Planned "Credibility" Actions	"Roadblock" or Obstacle	"Bust-up" Action

Establishing Credibility

4.17
Team Feedback

Review the following "credibility" statements. Based on your manager's actions, jot down your responses to each question. Share your responses with the team to create an overall team response for each question.

"Credibility" Statements	Response
What people talk about when you're not around is…	
We only have "half the scoop" on…	
Give it to us straight about…	
Your mouth and feet go in opposite direction on…	
You didn't follow through on…	
You "walked-the-talk" on…	
You seemed very credible when…	

Establishing Credibility

4.18
Commitment Log

Record your commitments below, identifying who the action is for and when it is due. For each action, rate the level of completion you achieve.

Level of Completion	Rating
You didn't do what you said you would	0
You completed the action, but not when you said you would	5
You completed the action when you said you would	10

Commitment	Individual/Group	Due Date	Completion Rating

Show Caring

Take action to show your employees you care about them as individuals

Show Caring

48 Hours

5.1 Talk-it-Up!
Tell your manager, team, and peers you plan to improve your "caring" skills

5.2 Benefit Analysis
Determine whether improving your "caring" skills will be valuable for yourself and others

5.3 Caring Profile
Evaluate how well you care for your team members

5.4 Caring Guide
Post a reminder to take action to show you care

7 Days

5.5 Two 4 U: Ideas for Improvement
Ask others for two ideas to improve your "caring" skills

5.6 Tracking Chart
Create a tracking chart to capture your "caring" progress

5.7 Caring Action Grid
Outline what you will do to show you care about each team member

5.8 Show You Care
Increase the actions you take to show you care about your employees

30 Days

5.9 Team Discussion
Facilitate a team discussion to improve your "caring" skills

5.10 Feedback for Me
Receive feedback on your "caring" actions

5.11 Learning Lunch
Schedule lunch with each team member to learn more about them

5.12 Personal Picture
Team members illustrate their personal experiences

5.13 Personal Purchase
Team members purchase something personal for their workspace

90 Days

5.14 Mini-Assessment
Assess your "caring" progress

5.15 Bust-up the Roadblocks
Identify the obstacles and hurdles preventing you from improving your "caring" skills

5.16 About Us Agenda
Build an agenda item into each staff meeting to discuss personal events

5.17 Caring Decision Criteria
Apply the caring criteria to decisions impacting your team members

Show Caring
48 Hours

Prep Time
5 minutes

Action Time
15 minutes

5.1
Talk-it-Up!
Tell your manager, team, and peers you plan to improve your caring skills

Identify the individuals and/or groups who will be most impacted by a change in your caring skills and share your desire to improve your capabilities.

Step 1: In a team meeting, share your desire to improve your caring capabilities. Be sure to discuss the following:
- Explain "why" you have chosen to improve your caring skills
- Describe how an increase in performance will help you, the organization, and others
- Outline what you actions you plan to take to impact your capabilities

Step 2: Solicit the groups' help and feedback. Ask them to support your development by focusing on your caring actions from this point forward (not what you did in the past). Ask them to give you feedback on what you are doing well and what you need to improve.

Note: *Talk-it-Up!* is best done face-to-face, however, you can also *Talk-it-Up!* during a conference call or via email.

Show Caring
48 Hours

Prep Time **5 minutes**   *Action Time* **10 minutes**

Download electronic copy:
www.keeppeople.com/book/5.2.dot

5.2
Benefit Analysis
Determine whether improving your caring skills will be valuable for yourself and others

Complete a *Benefit Analysis* to determine whether improving your caring skills will be valuable for yourself and others.

Step 1: Identify the key individuals and/or groups who will be most impacted by a change in your caring skills. Record their names on the **Benefit Analysis Square** (page 177).

Step 2: For each individual or group, answer the following question:

  "If you improve your caring capabilities, what benefits will be experienced by the individual or group?"

Identify two benefits for each individual or group, and record your responses on the *Benefit Analysis Square*.

Step 3: After completing the *Benefit Analysis Square*, determine whether the benefits of improving your caring capabilities outweigh the time and energy needed to improve your performance.

- If YES, move forward and take action to improve your caring capabilities
- If NO, select another manager capability to improve

Example

Your Employees
1. My team members will feel I genuinely care about them as individuals—not just as employees.
2. My employees will enjoy working for me <u>and</u> our team.

Show Caring
48 Hours

Prep Time **5 minutes** *Action Time* **15 minutes**

Download electronic copy:
www.keeppeople.com/book/5.3.pdf

5.3
Caring Profile
Evaluate how well you care for your team members

Assess how well you handled a personal event experienced by a team member in the last 60 days.

Step 1: Identify a team member who experienced a personal event in the last 60 days. Record the event on the **Caring Profile** (page 178).

A personal event may be a situation presenting a challenge for the team member, a personal struggle, or an extremely emotional situation for the team member.

Step 2: Review the Caring Profile Actions. Based on your own perception, determine what level of "caring" you offered the team member for each Caring Profile Action.

Step 3: Based on your responses, identify two actions you will take in the future to increase the level of caring you show your team members.

Example

Caring Profile Action	Level of Caring				
	Low	Low-Med	Medium	Med-High	High
LISTENING *I focused on listening to what my team member had to say, versus focusing on what I wanted to say*	○	○	○	●	○
SHARING AND DISCLOSING *I disclosed something about myself related to the situation*	○	●	○	○	○

Show Caring
48 Hours

Prep Time: 5 minutes
Action Time: 5 minutes/day

Download electronic copy:
www.keeppeople.com/book/5.4.pdf

5.4
Caring Guide
Post a reminder to take action to show you care

Post the *Caring Guide* in your work space to act as a reminder of the actions needed to show caring towards your team members.

Step 1: Print and cut out the **Caring Guide** (page 179).

Step 2: Post the *Caring Guide* in your work space in an area that is visible to you throughout the day.

Step 3: Each day, review the *Caring Guide* as a reminder of the actions which impact the level of caring you show your team members.

CARING GUIDE
LISTEN Focus on listening to team members versus focusing on what to say
SHARE AND DISCLOSE Share and disclose information about yourself
ACCEPT Listen to others without judging their thoughts and feelings
ACT When necessary, help your team members adjust their workload or work situation
BE SENSITIVE Treat situations with sensitivity and confidentiality
TREAT PEOPLE DIFFERENTLY Treat people differently because each person has unique needs
SHOW CONCERN Make time to show concern when employees are working through a difficult situation

Show Caring
7 Days

Prep Time **5 minutes** *Action Time* **60 minutes**

Download electronic copy:
www.keeppeople.com/book/5.5.dot

5.5
Two 4 U: Ideas for Improvement
Ask others for two ideas to improve your caring skills

Using the wisdom and experience from others, generate as many ideas as possible to improve your caring capabilities.

Step 1: Identify up to 5 people who have excellent caring skills.

Step 2: Ask each person the following question:

"I'm trying to improve my caring skills, do you have two ideas for how I can improve my capabilities?"

Step 3: Record each person's ideas on the **Two 4 U** worksheet (page 180).

Step 4: Once you gathered ideas from each person, review the suggestions and circle the top three ideas you think will help the most.

Step 5: For your top three ideas, identify the next steps you will take to implement the idea.

Step 6: Thank the individuals who gave you the development ideas and share what actions you plan to take to improve your caring capabilities.

Show Caring
7 Days

Prep Time **5 minutes**   *Action Time* **15 minutes**

Download electronic copy:
www.keeppeople.com/book/5.6.dot

5.6
Tracking Chart
Create a tracking chart to capture your caring progress

Each Friday capture what you actually completed during the week to improve your caring skills.

Step 1: Each Friday, identify and record the actions you took to improve your performance on the **Tracking Chart** (page 181).

Step 2: For each action, grade your performance based on how well you think you performed on the action, as well as considering feedback you may have received from others.

A = Excellent; B = Good; C = Average; D = Poor; F = Failing

Step 3: Based on your performance, identify one improvement action you will implement the following week.

Step 4: After completing the *Tracking Chat* ask yourself the following questions:
- Am I really taking actions to improve?
- Are my actions having the desired impact on my caring capabilities?

Example

Week	Caring Actions	Grade
September 8	Told Andrew to leave early so he could attend his daughter's soccer game	A
	Did not take the time to listen to Greg when he expressed concern about his workload	F
	Spent 20 minutes talking to Karen about moving her mother into a nursing home	B
Improvement Actions • Schedule a one-to-one with Greg • Ask Roger to speak with Karen regarding the steps he took to place his mother in a nursing home		

165

Show Caring
7 Days

Prep Time **5 minutes** *Action Time* **30 minutes**

Download electronic copy:
www.keeppeople.com/book/5.7.dot

5.7
Caring Action Grid
Outline what you will do to show you care about each team member

Identify specific actions you will take to show you care about each of your team members as a person—not just as an employee working for the organization.

Step 1: Record the names of your team members on the **Caring Action Grid** (page 182).

Step 2: For each team member, identify one action you will take to show you care about him or her as a person—not just as an employee working for the organization.

Determine what you can do to:
- Disclose information about yourself and learn about your employees
- Listen to your employees versus judging their thoughts and feelings
- Treat your employees differently to meet their individual needs
- Show empathy to your team members
- Help your team members resolve a difficult situation or offer solutions to a problem they are facing
- Learn about your employees' families, hobbies, special interests, etc.

Step 3: Record the actions on the *Caring Action Grid*.

Example

Team Member	Caring Actions
Amanda	Schedule lunch with Amanda to learn more about her
Courtney	Reduce Courtney's non-essential tasks/deliverables to help alleviate the stress the ALPHA Project creates
Matthew	Tell Matthew to come in 30 minutes later each morning until his newborn baby is sleeping better

Show Caring
7 Days

Prep Time **10 minutes** *Action Time* **TBD**

Download electronic copy:
www.keeppeople.com/book/5.8.dot

5.8 Show You Care

Increase the actions you take to show you care about your employees

Select specific actions you will implement for your team members to show you care.

Step 1: Review the caring actions on the **Show You Care** worksheet (page 183). Circle or highlight the actions you will implement with your team members.

Step 2: As you complete an action, record the team member's name and date you performed the action.

Step 3: Each week, tally the number of actions you took to show caring week.

Note: You can keep a record of the caring actions you implement for each team member (copy the worksheet for each team member), or you can keep one record for the entire team.

Show Caring
30 Days

Prep Time
5 minutes

Action Time
45 minutes

5.9
Team Discussion
Facilitate a team discussion to improve your caring skills

Solicit ideas from your team to improve your caring capabilities, and identify a way to receive immediate feedback as you implement your caring actions.

Step 1: In a team meeting share "why" you want to improve your caring skills, and share your thoughts about the importance of caring.

Step 2: Ask your team members to share how they think your caring capabilities impact the team and individual team members.

Step 3: Ask the team to brainstorm actions you can take to improve your caring skills.

Step 4: With the team, identify a way for team members to cue you when your actions are consistent, as well as inconsistent with the desired caring behaviors.

Try pick two hand gestures, statements, or signals to indicate when the new caring behaviors are happening and when they're not.

For example, team members may say *"Right on!"* when your behaviors are consistent, and *"Take a step back"* when your behaviors are inconsistent. Teams members may also use a hand gesture such as "thumbs-up" or "thumbs-down".

Show Caring
30 Days

Prep Time
5 minutes

Action Time
2 hours

Download electronic copy:
www.keeppeople.com/book/5.10.dot

5.10
Feedback for Me
Receive feedback on your caring actions

Solicit feedback on the actions you have taken to improve your caring capabilities.

Step 1: Identify up to 5 people who can give you feedback on your caring actions, and send them the following email:

> *I have chosen to take action to improve my caring skills and would like some help from you. In the next 30 to 45 days, I'd like to follow-up with you to receive feedback on my "caring" performance. When we talk, I will ask you the following questions:*
> 1. *What caring actions have you seen me perform?*
> 2. *What impact have my actions created for individuals, the team, and/or the organization?*
> 3. *What improvement ideas do you have for me?*
>
> *Thank you for your help. I look forward to speaking with you soon.*

Step 2: Identify a follow-up date when you will ask each person for feedback. Record the date on the **Feedback for Me** worksheet (page 184).

Step 3: At the time of your follow-up dates, schedule a 15 minute discussion with each person to receive feedback on your caring actions.

Step 4: After receiving feedback, record the feedback on the *Feedback for Me* worksheet. Be sure to thank each person for his or her time and willingness to provide you feedback on your caring actions.

Step 5: Based on the feedback you received, think about the following:
- What caring actions do I need to do more of?
- What actions do I need to do less of?
- What additional actions should I integrate into my caring improvement plan?

Show Caring
30 Days

Prep Time **5 minutes** *Action Time* **60 minutes/ employee**

5.11
Learning Lunch
Schedule lunch with each team member to learn more about them

Schedule a lunch with each team member to learn more about them as individuals, not just as employees who work for you.

Step 1: Schedule a lunch with each team member.

Step 2: During lunch, discuss the topics below. Be sure to share information about yourself first, and then ask your team member to discuss the topic.

Discussion Topics:
- Your career and the professional skills you want to develop
- Family, friends, hobbies, and interests
- Personal situations (what's going on, and how can the other person help)

Note:
- It will be important for you to share information first—show you are willing to disclose information and take a risk. This will increase the team member's willingness to share.

- If it is difficult to schedule all of your team members for lunch. Schedule a few to begin with, perform the *Learning Lunches,* and then schedule some more.

Show Caring
30 Days

Prep Time **5 minutes**   *Action Time* **90 minutes**

Download electronic copy:
www.keeppeople.com/book/5.12.dot

5.12
Personal Picture
Team members illustrate their personal experiences

Use the *Personal Picture* to help you and your team members get to know each other better.

Step 1: In a team meeting, give the **Personal Picture** (page 185) worksheet to each team member.

Step 2: Team members should silently think about the statements on the worksheet and identify a personal experience to describe each statement.

Step 3: Team members draw a picture (using markers or crayons) in each box to illustrate their personal experiences.

Step 4: Each team member takes a turn to share and describe his or her *Personal Picture* to the team.

Example

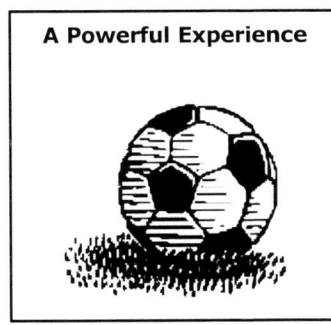

A Powerful Experience	A Personal Skill or Hobby	A Work Success
"Coaching a 'Special Olympics' team."	 "I can name all of our state's flowers—I'm a great person to take on a hike."	 "Streamlining our client screening process."

171

Center for Talent Retention © 2001-2005

Show Caring
30 Days

Prep Time
20 minutes

Action Time
60 minutes

5.13
Personal Purchase
Team members purchase something personal for their workspace

Give your team members a small budget to purchase something personal for their workspace.

Step 1: Based on your budget, determine a monetary amount you can give to each of your team members to purchase something personal for their workspace (e.g., $25 to $50)

Step 2: During a team meeting, introduce the *Personal Purchase* to your team members. Team members should purchase an item for their workspace that has personal meaning to the team member and is for the team member to keep.

Step 3: At a designated team meeting, team members should bring their *Personal Purchase* to the meeting to share it with the team and describe the personal meaning the item represents for the team member.

Show Caring
90 Days

Prep Time **10 minutes**   *Action Time* **30 minutes**

Download electronic copy:
www.keeppeople.com/book/5.14.pdf

5.14
Mini-Assessment
Assess your caring performance progress

Determine if your caring actions are perceived as more effective.

45 Days Before the Mini-Assessment:
Step 1: Identify the individuals and/or groups who will be most impacted by a change in your caring capabilities and share your desire to improve your caring skills.

Step 2: Explain "why" you have chosen to improve your caring capabilities. Describe how an increase in performance will help you, the organization, and others.

Step 3: Solicit their help and feedback. Ask the individuals to support your development by observing your actions for 45 days. Tell them at the end of the 45 days you will give them a *Mini-Assessment* to evaluate your caring actions.

The Mini-Assessment:
Step 4: After 45 days, give a copy of the **Mini-Assessment** (page 186) to the individuals you asked to observe your behaviors—ask them to complete the *Mini-Assessment* honestly.

Step 5: Request the individuals return the assessment to you when they are finished.

Step 6: Summarize your results for each statement. Where do you have strengths and weaknesses?

Step 7: Identify actions you will take based on your *Mini-Assessment* results.

Step 8: Share these actions with the individuals who gave you feedback and thank them for their help.

Show Caring
90 Days

Prep Time **5 minutes** *Action Time* **10 minutes**

Download electronic copy:
www.keeppeople.com/book/5.15.dot

5.15
Bust-up the Roadblocks
Identify the obstacles and hurdles preventing you from improving your caring skills

Identify why you may not be taking action to improve your caring skills, and/or determine why the actions you have taken are not having the desired impact.

Step 1: Record your current and planned caring actions on the **Bust-up the Roadblocks** worksheet (page 187).

Step 2: Review each action and determine if a "roadblock" or obstacle is preventing you from implementing a planned action or preventing a current action from creating its desired impact.

Step 3: Based on the "roadblock", identify "bust-up" actions you can take to eliminate or manage the roadblock.

Example

Current and Planned Caring Actions	"Roadblock" or Obstacle	"Bust-up" Action
I plan to perform a Learning Lunch with each team member in the next 6 weeks.	I don't have the time to meet with all my team members for a Learning Lunch within the next 6 weeks.	In the next 6 weeks I will meet with team members who I don't know well or those who are dealing with difficult work or personal situations. Once I meet with these team members, I'll schedule additional Learning Lunches.

Show Caring
90 Days

Prep Time **10 minutes** *Action Time* **10 minutes**

5.16
About Us Agenda
Build an agenda item into each staff meeting to discuss personal events

Keep your team members connected by building in 10 minutes into each staff meeting to discuss personal events.

Step 1: Build a 10 minute "standing agenda item" into each staff meeting to discuss team members' personal events.

Step 2: During the agenda item, find out what is happening in team members' lives, such as new homes, kid activities, weekend activities, etc. Use this time to check in with team members and get status updates on previously discussed events.

Show Caring
90 Days

Prep Time **10 minutes**   *Action Time* **TBD**

Download electronic copy:
www.keeppeople.com/book/5.17.pdf

5.17
Caring Decision Criteria
Apply the caring criteria to decisions impacting your team members

For 60 days, apply the *Caring Decision Criteria* to decisions impacting your team members.

Step 1: Record the decisions you must make that impact your team members on the **Caring Decision Criteria** worksheet (page 188).

Step 2: For each decision, review the *Caring Decision Criteria* and determine whether your answer is "Yes" or "No" to each criteria.

Step 3: If you answered "No" to one or more questions, identify actions you must take to say "Yes" to all of the criteria.

Example

		CARING DECISION CRITERIA
		**UNDERSTAND** Do I really understand how this decision will impact my employees?		**LISTEN** Have I taken steps to actively listen to the people who will be impacted by this decision?		**SHOW CONCERN** Have I taken steps to show I am concerned about the people who will be impacted by this decision?		**INDIVIDUALITY** Have I treated people differently because each person has unique needs?
DECISION: Reassign the BETA Project to Greg, Jen, and Stacey	Yes	No	Yes	No	Yes	No	Yes	No
ACTION: Alan is disappointed and confused about losing his BETA Project deliverables. Meet with Alan to discuss the rationale for the reassignment, identify his strengths and weaknesses, and determine the type of work he would like to do next.		

Show Caring

5.2
Benefit Analysis Square

For each individual or group, answer the following question:

"If you improve your caring skills, what benefits will be experienced by the individual or group?"

Identify two benefits for each individual or group, and record your responses below.

Determine whether the benefits of improving your "caring" skills outweigh the time and energy needed to improve your performance.

- If YES, move forward and take action to improve your "caring" skills
- If NO, select another manager capability to improve

Yourself	Your Manager	Your Employees
1.	1.	1.
2.	2.	2.

Your Peers & Co-Workers		Key Customers & Clients
1.	**Benefits**	1.
2.		2.

Your Significant Other/Family	Other _____	Other _____
1.	1.	1.
2.	2.	2.

Show Caring

5.3 Caring Profile

Identify a team member who experienced a personal event in the last 60 days. Record the event below

Review the Caring Profile Actions. Based on your own perception, determine what level of "caring" you offered the team member for each Caring Profile Action. Based on your responses, identify two actions you will take in the future to increase the level of caring you show your team members.

Team Member	Personal Event

Caring Profile Action	Level of Caring				
	Low	Low-Med	Medium	Med-High	High
LISTENING I focused on listening to what my team member had to say, versus focusing on what I wanted to say	○	○	○	○	○
SHARING AND DISCLOSING I disclosed something about myself related to the situation	○	○	○	○	○
ACCEPTING I did not judge my team member for his or her thoughts and feelings	○	○	○	○	○
ACTIONS I took action to adjust the team member's work and work environment	○	○	○	○	○
SENSITIVITY I treated the team member's situation with sensitivity and the confidentiality required	○	○	○	○	○
UNIQUE NEEDS I addressed the team member's unique needs	○	○	○	○	○
CONCERN I made the time to show concern when the team member was working through the situation	○	○	○	○	○

FUTURE ACTIONS	
1	
2	

Show Caring

5.4
Caring Guide

Print and cut out the *Caring Guide*. Post the *Caring Guide* in your work space in an area that is visible to you throughout the day. Each day, review the *Caring Guide* as a reminder of the actions which impact the level of caring you show your team members.

CARING GUIDE

LISTEN
Focus on listening to team members
versus focusing on what to say

SHARE AND DISCLOSE
Share and disclose information about yourself

ACCEPT
Listen to others without judging
their thoughts and feelings

ACT
When necessary, help your team members adjust
their workload or work situation

BE SENSITIVE
Treat situations with sensitivity and confidentiality

TREAT PEOPLE DIFFERENTLY
Treat people differently because each
person has unique needs

SHOW CONCERN
Make time to show concern when employees are
working through a difficult situation

Show Caring

5.5
Two 4 U

Identify up to 5 people who have excellent "caring" skills and ask each person the following question:

"I'm trying to improve my "caring" skills, do you have two ideas for how I can improve my caring capabilities?"

Record each person's ideas below. Once you gathered ideas from each person, review the suggestions and circle the top three ideas you think will help the most.

For your top three ideas, identify the next steps you will take to implement the idea.

Individual	Idea #1	Idea #2	Next Steps

Show Caring

5.6
Tracking Chart

Each Friday, identify and record the actions you took to improve your performance. For each action, grade your performance based on how well you think you performed on the action, as well as considering feedback you may have received from others.

A = Excellent; B = Good; C = Average; D = Poor; F = Failing

Based on your performance, identify one improvement action you will implement the following week.

Week	Caring Actions	Grade

Improvement Action:

Week	Caring Actions	Grade

Improvement Action:

Week	Caring Actions	Grade

Improvement Action:

Show Caring

5.7
Caring Action Grid

Record the names of your team members below. For each team member, identify one action you will take to show you care about him or her as a person—not just as an employee working for the organization.

Team Member	Caring Action

Show Caring

5.8
Show You Care

Circle or highlight the actions you will implement with your team. As you complete an action, record the team member's name and date you completed the action.

25 Caring Actions		Team Member	Date
1	Send a note to an employee's significant other describing how much you value and appreciate the employee's contributions		
2	Leave a surprise (e.g., candy bar, balloon, trophy, certificate of achievement) on an employee's chair—be sure to include a note of appreciation		
3	Help an employee handle a personal situation (e.g., listen, rearrange the employee's work situation, identify outside resources)		
4	Celebrate an "out-of-work" accomplishment (e.g., college degree, pilot's license, wedding, certification)		
5	Ask an employee about his or her family, weekend activities, hobbies, etc.		
6	Discuss the positive impact of an employee's actions on a conference call		
7	Create a team calendar with birthdays and employment anniversaries		
8	Bake cookies for your employees		
9	Order-in lunch for an employee who is working hard and does not have time to get lunch		
10	Tell a story about a special achievement of the team or team member		
11	Plan an event to "blow-off" steam, unwind, or reduce stress		
12	Personally congratulate an employee for a job well done by shaking his or her hand		
13	Ask your manager or the leader of your workgroup to call an employee to thank the employee for a job well done		
14	Follow-up with an employee regarding a difficult personal situation—find out how the employee is doing and ask how you can help		
15	Eliminate a task from an overwhelmed employee—complete the task yourself		
16	Thank an employee for a task or job which is "taken for granted"		
17	When introducing a peer, new team member, or co-worker to an employee, tell the person about one of the employee's strengths		
18	Tell an employee about one action he or she is really good at, and describe the impact the action has on the team		
19	When you hear a positive remark about an employee, share it with the person as soon as possible		
20	Leave a post-it note on the employee's desk saying, "Thanks for being here—We would not be able to accomplish _____ without you."		
21	Identify where you need to "rebalance" deliverables or where you need to "pair-up" employees		
22	Take an employee out to lunch—talk about anything BUT work		
23	Schedule one-to-one meetings with each of your employees to "check-in" and see how everything is going		
24	Walk around and visit with each employee		
25	Tell an employee what you like about him or her—share this information with others		

Show Caring

5.10
Feedback for Me

Identify up to 5 people who can give you feedback on your "caring" actions. Determine when you will follow-up with each person and record the date below.

After receiving feedback, record the feedback from each person.

Based on the feedback you received, think about the following:
- What "caring" actions do I need to do more of?
- What actions do I need to do less of?
- What additional actions should I integrate into my "caring" improvement plan?

Name	Follow-Up Date	Feedback		
		What "caring" actions have you seen me perform?	*What impact have my actions created for individuals, the team, and/or the organization?*	*What improvement ideas do you have for me?*

Center for Talent Retention © 2000-2005

Show Caring

5.12
Personal Picture

Silently think about the statements below and identify a personal experience to describe each statement.

Draw a picture (using markers or crayons) in each box to illustrate your personal experience.

Where I Grew Up	**My Favorite Vacation**	**The Place I'd Like to Retire**
A Powerful Experience	**A Personal Skill or Hobby**	**A Favorite Family Member**
My First Job	**A Work Success**	**My Career Goals**

Show Caring

5.14
Mini-Assessment

A little over a month ago I began improving my "caring" capabilities. Please help me gauge my performance by taking 5 minutes to answer a few questions. Please return the assessment with the enclosed envelope.

Thank you for your feedback!

Caring Mini-Assessment

Please evaluate my improvement in the area of "caring".

For each of the following statements, circle the level of change you have noticed in my actions <u>in the last 45 Days</u>.

Am I MORE or LESS effective on the following...

Less Effective	No Perceivable Change	More Effective	Not Applicable
-2 -1	0 +1	+2	NA

My actions show I genuinely care about you as a person

    -2   -1   0   +1   +2   NA

I help team members learn more about each other

    -2   -1   0   +1   +2   NA

I take the time to learn how you are doing

    -2   -1   0   +1   +2   NA

I often stop by your work area to say hello

    -2   -1   0   +1   +2   NA

I take action to help you with personal situations

    -2   -1   0   +1   +2   NA

What else can I do to improve the level of care and concern I show you?

_____

_____

_____

_____

5.15
Bust-up the Roadblocks

Record your current and planned "caring" actions below. Review each action and determine if a "roadblock" or obstacle is preventing you from implementing a planned action or preventing a current action from creating its desired impact. Based on the "roadblock", identify "bust-up" actions you can take to eliminate or manage the roadblock.

Current and Planned "Caring" Actions	"Roadblock" or Obstacle	"Bust-up" Action

Show Caring

5.17
Caring Decision Criteria

Record the decisions you must make that impact your team members below. For each decision, review the *Caring Decision Criteria* and determine whether your answer is "Yes" or "No" to each criteria. If you answered "No" to one or more questions, identify actions you must take to say "Yes" to all of the criteria.

DECISION	CARING DECISION CRITERIA							
	UNDERSTAND Do I really understand how this decision will impact my employees?		**LISTEN** Have I taken steps to actively listen to the people who will be impacted by this decision?		**SHOW CONCERN** Have I taken steps to show I am concerned about the people who will be impacted by this decision?		**INDIVIDUALITY** Have I treated people differently because each person has unique needs?	
DECISION:	Yes	No	Yes	No	Yes	No	Yes	No
ACTION:								
DECISION:	Yes	No	Yes	No	Yes	No	Yes	No
ACTION:								
DECISION:	Yes	No	Yes	No	Yes	No	Yes	No
ACTION:								
DECISION:	Yes	No	Yes	No	Yes	No	Yes	No
ACTION:								

Communication

Create an environment to encourage comfortable two-way dialogue and the exchanging of ideas

Communication

48 Hours

6.1 Talk-it-Up!
Tell your manager, team, and peers you plan to improve your "communication" skills

6.2 Benefit Analysis
Determine whether improving your "communication" skills will be valuable for yourself and others

6.3 My Listening Skills
Evaluate your listening skills

6.4 Get-the-Facts
Post a reminder to find out the facts before taking action

7 Days

6.5 Two 4 U: Ideas for Improvement
Ask others for two ideas to improve your "communication" skills

6.6 Tracking Chart
Create a tracking chart to capture your "communication" progress

6.7 Assess My Communication
Receive input on your communication skills

6.8 Communication Action Grid
Take action to improve your communication with each of your team members

30 Days

6.9 Team Discussion
Facilitate a team discussion to improve your "communication" skills

6.10 Feedback for Me
Receive feedback on your "communication" actions

6.11 One-to-One Dialogue
Create a rich, robust dialogue with your team members

6.12 Hot Seat
Create an environment of open communication with your team

6.13 Communication Puzzle
Keep track of the communication actions you take with your team members

90 Days

6.14 Mini-Assessment
Assess your "communication" progress

6.15 Bust-up the Roadblocks
Identify the obstacles and hurdles preventing you from improving your "communication" skills

6.16 Big Ideas
Solicit improvement ideas from your team members

6.17 External Practice
Practice communication actions outside of work

Communication
48 Hours

Prep Time **5 minutes** *Action Time* **15 minutes**

6.1
Talk-it-Up!
Tell your manager, team, and peers you plan to improve your communication skills

Identify the individuals and/or groups who will be most impacted by a change in your communication skills and share your desire to improve your capabilities.

Step 1: In a team meeting, share your desire to improve your communication capabilities. Be sure to discuss the following:
- Explain "why" you have chosen to improve your communication skills
- Describe how an increase in performance will help you, the organization, and others
- Outline what you actions you plan to take to impact your capabilities

Step 2: Solicit the groups' help and feedback. Ask them to support your development by focusing on your communication actions from this point forward (not what you did in the past). Ask them to give you feedback on what you are doing well and what you need to improve.

Note: *Talk-it-Up!* is best done face-to-face, however, you can also *Talk-it-Up!* during a conference call or via email.

Communication
48 Hours

Prep Time **5 minutes**   *Action Time* **10 minutes**

Download electronic copy:
www.keeppeople.com/book/6.2.dot

6.2
Benefit Analysis
Determine whether improving your communication skills will be valuable for yourself and others

Complete a *Benefit Analysis* to determine whether improving your communication skills will be valuable for yourself and others.

Step 1: Identify the key individuals and/or groups who will be most impacted by a change in your communication skills. Record their names on the **Benefit Analysis Square** (page 211).

Step 2: For each individual or group, answer the following question:

"*If you improve* your communication *capabilities, what benefits will be experienced by the individual or group?*"

Identify two benefits for each individual or group, and record your responses on the *Benefit Analysis Square*.

Step 3: After completing the *Benefit Analysis Square*, determine whether the benefits of improving your communication capabilities outweigh the time and energy needed to improve your performance.

- If YES, move forward and take action to improve your communication skills
- If NO, select another manager capability to improve

Example

Your Employees
1. My employees will be comfortable asking me questions and discussing important issues.
2. My employees will know I understand their position and really value their input.

Communication
48 Hours

Prep Time **5 minutes**   *Action Time* **15 minutes**

Download electronic copy:
www.keeppeople.com/book/6.3.pdf

6.3
My Listening Skills
Evaluate your listening skills

Determine how well you listen to others.

Step 1: Review the "listening actions" on the **My Listening Skills** worksheet (page 212).

Step 2: For each "listening action", think about the last 3 times you listened to a team member, peer, or friend, and determine which rating best describes your past actions and behaviors. Record your score.

Step 3: Total your "listening action" scores, and review your rating.

Step 4: Based on your rating, identify what actions you can take to improve your listening skills.

Example

Listening Action	Never -10	Rarely -5	Sometimes +5	Often +10	Score
I made eye contact with the person	○	○	●	○	+5
I acknowledged the person through verbal and non-verbal gestures	○	●	○	○	-5
I paraphrased (summarized/restated) what the person said	○	○	○	●	+10

Communication
48 Hours

Prep Time
5 minutes

Action Time
5 minutes/day

Download electronic copy:
www.keeppeople.com/book/6.4.pdf

6.4
Get-the-Facts
Post a reminder to find out the facts before taking action

Post the *Get-the-Facts* in your work space to act as a reminder to "get-the-facts" before taking action or making judgments.

Step 1: Print and cut out the **Get-the-Facts** guide (page 213).

Step 2: Post the *Get-the-Facts Guide* in your work space in an area that is visible to you throughout the day.

Step 3: Each day, review the *Get-the-Facts Guide* as a reminder of the actions needed before taking action or making judgments.

Get-the Facts

- Do I know all "sides" of the issue?
- Who else should I talk with before taking action?
- What facts do I know?
- What facts do I need to know?
- When do I <u>really</u> have to take action?

Communication
7 Days

Prep Time **5 minutes** *Action Time* **60 minutes**

Download electronic copy:
www.keeppeople.com/book/6.5.dot

6.5
Two 4 U: Ideas for Improvement
Ask others for two ideas to improve your communication skills

Using the wisdom and experience from others, generate as many ideas as possible to improve your communication capabilities.

Step 1: Identify up to 5 people who have excellent communication skills.

Step 2: Ask each person the following question:

"I'm trying to improve my communication skills, do you have two ideas for how I can improve my capabilities?"

Step 3: Record each person's ideas on the **Two 4 U** worksheet (page 214).

Step 4: Once you gathered ideas from each person, review the suggestions and circle the top three ideas you think will help the most.

Step 5: For your top three ideas, identify the next steps you will take to implement the idea.

Step 6: Thank the individuals who gave you the development ideas and share what actions you plan to take to improve your communication capabilities.

Communication
7 Days

Prep Time 5 minutes
Action Time 10 minutes

Download electronic copy:
www.keeppeople.com/book/6.6.dot

6.6
Tracking Chart
Create a tracking chart to capture your communication progress

Each Friday capture what you actually completed during the week to improve your communication skills.

Step 1: Each Friday, identify and record the actions you took to improve your performance on the **Tracking Chart** (page 215).

Step 2: For each action, grade your performance based on how well you think you performed on the action, as well as considering feedback you may have received from others.

A = Excellent; B = Good; C = Average; D = Poor; F = Failing

Step 3: Based on your performance, identify one improvement action you will implement the following week.

Step 4: After completing the *Tracking Chat* ask yourself the following questions:
- Am I really taking actions to improve?
- Are my actions having the desired impact on my communication skills?

Example

Week	Communication Actions	Grade
July 20	Reviewed the *Get-the-Facts Guide* before talking to Chris about the lost customer order	B
	Asked Sam for his ideas regarding the implementation of the ROVER Project	A
	Focused on listening versus responding, when talking to Pat about customer concerns	B
Improvement Actions • Schedule one-to-ones with each employee		

199

Communication
7 Days

Prep Time
5 minutes

Action Time
60 minutes

6.7
Assess My Communication
Receive input on your communication skills

Ask your team members to evaluate how well you communicate with them.

Step 1: Send the following email to your team members:

I am currently working to improve my "communication" capabilities, and would like your help.

Please take five minutes to evaluate my communication skills by answering the following questions:

1. On a scale of 1 to 10 (1=I'm not interested in what others have to say; 10=I actively listen to your point of view <u>and</u> your ideas)
    - How would you rate my "day-to-day" communication actions?
2. When did I do a good job of asking for your ideas?
3. When did I do a good job of actively listening to you?
4. Do you believe I get-the-facts before making judgments and taking action?
    - In 20 words or less, explain <u>Why</u> or <u>Why Not</u>

Step 2: Follow-up with each team member (face-to-face or phone call) to discuss your communication with the team member. During the follow-up discussion, identify actions you will take to improve your communication with each team member.

Communication
7 Days

Prep Time **5 minutes** Action Time **TBD**

Download electronic copy:
www.keeppeople.com/book/6.8.dot

6.8
Communication Action Grid
Take action to improve your communication with each of your team members

Identify the actions you are willing to take to improve your communication with each of your team members.

Step 1: Record each of your team member's names on the **Communication Action Grid** (page 216).

Step 2: Review the communication categories. For each team member, identify at least one category you would like to do more for him or her.

Step 3: Outline the actions you will take to increase the quality of your communication for the team member.

Example

Team Member	COMFORTABLE TEAM MEMBER	LISTEN	ASK	GET-THE-FACTS
	The team member is comfortable asking you questions and discussing important issues	You actively listen to the team member and seek to understand the team member's points of view	You ask for the team member's ideas	You get the facts before making judgments or taking action
Kimberly			Kimberly is very knowledgeable about Product X —when I need to discuss Product X with a customer, I will ask for Kimberly's input first. I will meet with Kimberly to learn how she would improve our marketing materials.	

201
Center for Talent Retention © 2001-2005

Communication
30 Days

Prep Time **5 minutes** *Action Time* **45 minutes**

6.9
Team Discussion
Facilitate a team discussion to improve your communication skills

Solicit ideas from your team to improve your communication capabilities, and identify a way to receive immediate feedback as you implement your communication actions.

Step 1: In a team meeting share "why" you want to improve your communication skills, and share your thoughts about the importance of communication.

Step 2: Ask your team members to share how they think your communication capabilities impact the team and individual team members.

Step 3: Ask the team to brainstorm actions you can take to improve your communication skills.

Step 4: With the team, identify a way for team members to cue you when your actions are consistent, as well as inconsistent with the desired communication behaviors.

Try pick two hand gestures, statements, or signals to indicate when the new Communication behaviors are happening and when they're not.

For example, team members may say *"Right on!"* when your behaviors are consistent, and *"Take a step back"* when your behaviors are inconsistent. Teams members may also use a hand gesture such as "thumbs-up" or "thumbs-down".

Communication
30 Days

Prep Time
5 minutes

Action Time
2 hours

Download electronic copy:
www.keeppeople.com/book/6.10.dot

6.10
Feedback for Me
Receive feedback on your communication actions

Solicit feedback on the actions you have taken to improve your communication capabilities.

Step 1: Identify up to 5 people who can give you feedback on your communication actions, and send them the following email:

> *I have chosen to take action to improve my communication skills and would like some help from you. In the next 30 to 45 days, I'd like to follow-up with you to receive feedback on my "communication" performance. When we talk, I will ask you the following questions:*
> 1. *What communication actions have you seen me perform?*
> 2. *What impact have my actions created for individuals, the team, and/or the organization?*
> 3. *What improvement ideas do you have for me?*
>
> *Thank you for your help. I look forward to speaking with you soon.*

Step 2: Identify a follow-up date when you will ask each person for feedback. Record the date on the **Feedback for Me** worksheet (page 217).

Step 3: At the time of your follow-up dates, schedule a 15 minute discussion with each person to receive feedback on your communication actions.

Step 4: After receiving feedback, record the feedback on the *Feedback for Me* worksheet. Be sure to thank each person for his or her time and willingness to provide you feedback on your communication actions.

Step 5: Based on the feedback you received, think about the following:
- What communication actions do I need to do more of?
- What actions do I need to do less of?
- What additional actions should I integrate into my communication improvement plan?

Communication
30 Days

Prep Time **10 minutes**   *Action Time* **30 minutes/ employees**

Download electronic copy:
www.keeppeople.com/book/6.11.pdf
www.keeppeople.com/book/6.11a.pdf

6.11
One-to-One Dialogue
Create a rich, robust dialogue with your team members

One-to-One Dialogue is the foundation to engaging and retaining employees. It creates the opportunity to really understand what is "most critical" to team members, what it's really like for them right now, and what actions must be taken to ensure they engage in their work and stay with the organization.

Step 1: Review the **One-to-One Dialogue Guide** (page 218) to understand the *One-to-One Dialogue Components*.

Step 2: Schedule a *One-to-One Dialogue* with each team member and print the **One-to-One Dialogue** worksheet (page 219).

Step 3: With the team member perform the following:
1. Identify "The WHAT" and record it on the *One-to-One Dialogue* worksheet.
2. For "The WHAT" variables, discuss with the team member "WHY" they are "most critical".
3. Discuss "The REALITY" for each variables to identify what is it really like for the team member right now.
4. Determine "The ACTIONS" both you and the team member will take to maintain what is going well and positively impact what needs improvement.

Step 4: Be sure to touch base with the team member to see how the selected actions impacted the current situation. Determine if you and/or the team member must take additional actions to make an improvement.

Note: If it's too difficult to schedule all of your team members for a One-to-One Dialogue, start with a few team members, then schedule more as time allows.

Communication
30 Days

Prep Time
5 minutes

Action Time
60 minutes

6.12
Hot Seat
Create an environment of open communication with your team

Take the "heat" from your team members to create an environment of open communication.

Step 1: In a team meeting, give your team members two minutes to develop three questions they want answered.

Step 2: One at a time, each team member fires a question at you. You must respond within 30 seconds. Once you answer one question, move to the next employee. Go around the room until all the questions are answered.

Note: If you'd like, you can "pass" on a question and come back to it at the end of the *Hot Seat* session, or tell the team you will get the answer after the session and share it with them at a later time.

Communication
30 Days

Prep Time 20 minutes   **Action Time** TBD

Download electronic copy:
www.keeppeople.com/book/6.13.pdf
www.keeppeople.com/book/6.13a.pdf

6.13
Communication Puzzle
Keep track of the communication actions you take with your team members

Use the *Communicate Puzzle* to ensure you take action to improve your communication with each of your team members.

Step 1: Print the **Communication Cards** (page 220) for each team member. Cut out the cards, and give all four cards to each team member.

Step 2: Ask your team members to pay attention to your communication actions, and return each card once they "experience" you performing the communication action on the card.

Step 3: When you receive a card from a team member, check-off the card in the team member's column on the **Communication Action Chart** (page 221), recording the date you received the card.

Step 4: As you begin to receive the cards back from your team members, review the *Communication Action Chart* and think about the following questions:
- Is there one communication action you do more of or less of?
- Are you more effective at communicating with some team members versus others?
- Who do you need to improve your communication actions with?

See if you can get all four cards back from each team member within 30 days.

Communication
90 Days

Prep Time **10 minutes**   *Action Time* **30 minutes**

Download electronic copy:
www.keeppeople.com/book/6.14.pdf

6.14
Mini-Assessment
Assess your communication performance progress

Determine if your communication actions are perceived as more effective.

45 Days Before the Mini-Assessment:
Step 1: Identify the individuals and/or groups who will be most impacted by a change in your ccommunication capabilities and share your desire to improve your communication skills.

Step 2: Explain "why" you have chosen to improve your communication capabilities. Describe how an increase in performance will help you, the organization, and others.

Step 3: Solicit their help and feedback. Ask the individuals to support your development by observing your actions for 45 days. Tell them at the end of the 45 days you will give them a *Mini-Assessment* to evaluate your communication actions.

The Mini-Assessment:
Step 4: After 45 days, give a copy of the **Mini-Assessment** (page 222) to the individuals you asked to observe your behaviors—ask them to complete the *Mini-Assessment* honestly.

Step 5: Request the individuals return the assessment to you when they are finished.

Step 6: Summarize your results for each statement. Where do you have strengths and weaknesses?

Step 7: Identify actions you will take based on your *Mini-Assessment* results.

Step 8: Share these actions with the individuals who gave you feedback and thank them for their help.

Communication
90 Days

Prep Time **5 minutes**   *Action Time* **10 minutes**

Download electronic copy:
www.keeppeople.com/book/6.15.dot

6.15
Bust-up the Roadblocks
Identify the obstacles and hurdles preventing you from improving your communication skills

Identify why you may not be taking action to improve your communication skills, and/or determine why the actions you have taken are not having the desired impact.

Step 1: Record your current and planned communication actions on the **Bust-up the Roadblocks** worksheet (page 223).

Step 2: Review each action and determine if a "roadblock" or obstacle is preventing you from implementing a planned action or preventing a current action from creating its desired impact.

Step 3: Based on the "roadblock", identify "bust-up" actions you can take to eliminate or manage the roadblock.

Example

Current and Planned Communication Actions	"Roadblock" or Obstacle	"Bust-up" Action
I plan to perform a One-to-One Dialogue with each team member in the next 6 weeks.	I don't have the time to meet with all my team members for a One-to-One Dialogue within the next 6 weeks.	In the next 6 weeks I will meet with team members who are at risk of disengaging from their work or leaving the team. Once I meet with these team members, I'll schedule additional One-to-One Dialogues.

Communication
90 Days

Prep Time
10 minutes

Action Time
2 hours

6.16
Big Ideas
Solicit improvement ideas from your team members

Facilitate a team work session to brainstorm improvement ideas team members would like to implement within the team

Step 1: In a team meeting, describe the purpose of the *Big Ideas* work session. Be sure to mention the following:
- This is an opportunity to share your ideas to improve the team
- This is a brainstorming session—there are no bad ideas.

Step 2: With the team, brainstorm improvement ideas using the following categories to help brainstorm ideas.

People	The overall work experience for individual employees
Process	The methods and systems of the team and organization
Projects	Team or department assignments
Products	Organization products and services
Policies	The rules and guidelines which govern our organization

Step 3: Categorize each idea into one of three groups:
- **Great Idea**—Implement the idea with speed
- **Idea has Potential**—Further investigation is needed before taking action
- **Mixed Review**—Table the idea for now

Step 4: Assign an "Idea Sponsor" for each idea, identifying what actions will be taken and when they are due.

Step 5: Schedule the next *Big Ideas* meeting to review the progress on each idea, and add any new "big ideas". Determine how well the team followed through on their assigned actions, and determine what additional actions must be taken.

Communication
90 Days

Prep Time **10 minutes**   *Action Time* **TBD**

6.17
External Practice
Practice communication actions outside of work

Use outside organizations to practice building your "communication" capabilities.

Step 1: Think about the different groups and individuals you are involved in outside your work (your family, school boards, church, professional organizations, etc.).

Step 2: Choose one of these individuals or groups to practice "communication" actions with.

Step 3: Use the following questions to help you identify two actions you will take to practice "communicating" with others:

- *What can you do in the next meeting or interaction to seek out the opinions and ideas of others?*

- *What can you do get the facts before making judgments or taking action?*

- *What can you do to create a comfortable environment for others to ask you questions and discuss important issues?*

Step 4: Implement your identified actions.

Communication

6.2
Benefit Analysis Square

For each individual or group, answer the following question:

"If you improve your communication skills, what benefits will be experienced by the individual or group?"

Identify two benefits for each individual or group, and record your responses below.

Determine whether the benefits of improving your "communication" skills outweigh the time and energy needed to improve your performance.

- If YES, move forward and take action to improve your "communication" skills
- If NO, select another manager capability to improve

Yourself	Your Manager	Your Employees
1.	1.	1.
2.	2.	2.

Your Peers & Co-Workers		Key Customers & Clients
1.	**Benefits**	1.
2.		2.

Your Significant Other/Family	Other _____	Other _____
1.	1.	1.
2.	2.	2.

Center for Talent Retention © 2000-2005

Communication

6.3
My Listening Skills

Review the "listening actions" below. For each "listening action", think about the last 3 times you listened to a team member, peer, or friend, and determine which rating best describes your past actions and behaviors. Record your score.

Total your "listening action" scores, and review your rating. Based on your rating, identify what actions you can take to improve your listening skills.

Listening Action	Never -10	Rarely -5	Sometimes +5	Often +10	Score
I made eye contact with the person	○	○	○	○	
I acknowledged the person through verbal and non-verbal gestures	○	○	○	○	
I paraphrased (summarized/restated) what the person said	○	○	○	○	
I asked questions for clarification	○	○	○	○	
I focused on listening versus talking (80% listening, 20% talking)	○	○	○	○	
I waited until the person was finished describing the situation before I offered solutions	○	○	○	○	
I paid attention to the person's non-verbal behaviors	○	○	○	○	
I focused on understanding the person's statements versus formulating my responses	○	○	○	○	
I asked open-ended questions	○	○	○	○	
I understood the person's perspective on the situation	○	○	○	○	
				TOTAL	

Rating	
-100 to -50 points	**POOR:** *Your listening skills are very poor—take immediate action to improve your listening capabilities*
-49 to 0 points	**FAIR:** *Your listening skills are questionable—identify actions you will take to improve your listening capabilities*
+1 to +60 points	**GOOD:** *You are on your way to building good listening skills—continue to monitor your actions*
+61 to +100 points	**EXCELLENT:** *You have great listening skills—keep up the good work*

Communication

6.4
Get-the-Facts

Print and cut out the *Get-the-Facts Guide*. Post the *Get-the-Facts Guide* in your work space in an area that is visible to you throughout the day. Each day, review the *Get-the-Facts Guide* as a reminder of the actions needed before taking action or making judgments.

Get-the Facts

- Do I know all "sides" of the issue?
- Who else should I talk with before taking action?
- What facts do I know?
- What facts do I need to know?
- When do I <u>really</u> have to take action?

Communication

6.5
Two 4 U

Identify up to 5 people who have excellent "communication" skills and ask each person the following question:

"I'm trying to improve my "communication" skills, do you have two ideas for how I can improve my communication capabilities?"

Record each person's ideas below. Once you gathered ideas from each person, review the suggestions and circle the top three ideas you think will help the most.

For your top three ideas, identify the next steps you will take to implement the idea.

Individual	Idea #1	Idea #2	Next Steps

Communication

6.6
Tracking Chart

Each Friday, identify and record the actions you took to improve your performance. For each action, grade your performance based on how well you think you performed on the action, as well as considering feedback you may have received from others.

A = Excellent; B = Good; C = Average; D = Poor; F = Failing

Based on your performance, identify one improvement action you will implement the following week.

Week	Communication Actions	Grade

Improvement Action:

Week	Communication Actions	Grade

Improvement Action:

Week	Communication Actions	Grade

Improvement Action:

Communication

6.8
Communication Action Grid

Record each of your team member's names below. Review the communication categories. For each team member, identify at least one category you would like to do more for him or her. Outline the actions you will take to increase the quality of your communication for the team member.

Team Member	COMFORTABLE TEAM MEMBER The team member is comfortable asking you questions and discussing important issues	LISTEN You actively listen to the team member and seek to understand the team member's points of view	ASK You ask for the team member's ideas	GET-THE-FACTS You get the facts before making judgments or taking action

Communication

6.10
Feedback for Me

Identify up to 5 people who can give you feedback on your "communication" actions. Determine when you will follow-up with each person and record the date below.

After receiving feedback, record the feedback from each person.

Based on the feedback you received, think about the following:
- What "communication" actions do I need to do more of?
- What actions do I need to do less of?
- What additional actions should I integrate into my "communication" improvement plan?

Name	Follow-Up Date	Feedback		
		What "communication" actions have you seen me perform?	*What impact have my actions created for individuals, the team, and/or the organization?*	*What improvement ideas do you have for me?*

Communication

6.11
One-to-One Dialogue Guide

Use the *One-to-One Dialogue Guide* to help you conduct a rich, robust *One-to-One Dialogue* with your team members.

The Foundation
Engaging and retaining employees happens one person at-a-time. There is no easy way around it. If you want to engage your new hires, and keep your talented team members, you must take action at the individual level.

This is why One-to-One Dialogue is the foundation to engaging and retaining employees. It creates the opportunity for you to really understand what is "most critical" to your new hires, what it is really like for them right now, and what actions you both can take to increase the new hire's engagement and desire to stay.

One-to-One Dialogue Components
The One-to-One Dialogue process quickly and easily enables managers to understand what is "most critical" to new hires, what it is really like, and what actions both the manager and the new hire can take to maintain what's going well and positively impact what needs improvement

Let's take a look at the components of a great One-to-One Dialogue.

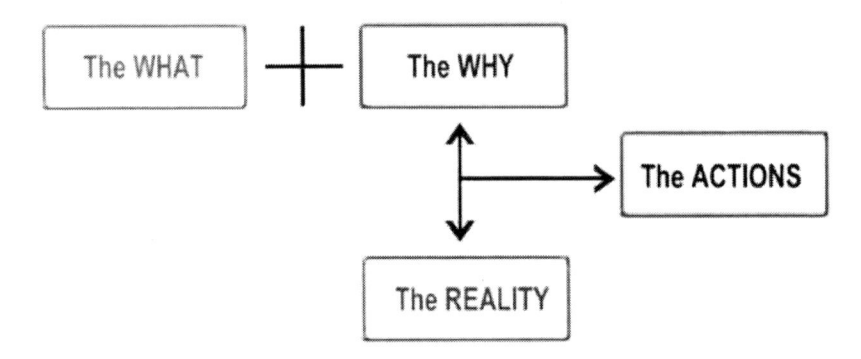

```
 The WHAT  ──┬──  The WHY
             │       │
             │       ├──▶ The ACTIONS
             │       ▼
             │    The REALITY
```

The What
The first component of One-to-One Dialogue is identifying what is "most critical" to your new hire.

The Why
The second component of One-to-One Dialogue is learning "why" the variable is critical to the new hire. Understanding "why" a variable is critical will help you assess the priority of the issue, as well as the surrounding circumstances.

The Reality
The third component of One-to-One Dialogue is learning what it is really like for the new hire right now. To take action and impact a new hire's "most critical" needs you must have a clear understanding of how well those "most critical" needs are currently being met.

The Actions
The final component of One-to-One Dialogue is identifying the actions you will take, as well as the actions your new hire will take to make a difference in the current situation.

It's true, a lot of the issues impacting employee performance and turnover are difficult to see. However, the One-to-One Dialogue process provides us an easy way to understand the What, the Why, the Reality, and the Actions for each new hire. It allows us to take action to engage and retain employees one person at-a-time—and as we know, this is the formula for success.

Will new hires take the risk?
At this point you may wonder if your new hire will tell you the truth. That is, will he or she tell you what is "most critical" and what it's really like right now?

Each of your new hires will feel comfortable sharing different concerns. Some may be willing to tell you what is really going on right away, while others may need to "test-the-water" first.

Some new hires provide "safe" answers to see how you will react to them, as well as how you react to other employees' concerns and issues. Realize you are being watched. Each new hire will watch how you respond to his or her initial concerns. If you are genuine and take action on the issues you can impact, new hires will feel comfortable sharing more and more.

Communication

6.11
One-to-One Dialogue Worksheet

Use this worksheet during the One-to-One Dialogue to capture the WHAT, WHY, REALITY, and ACTIONS for the team member's "most critical" variables. We recommend you select two variables to begin with. If times allows you can select another, or come back together for another *One-to-One Dialogue* to review additional variables.

Variable #1

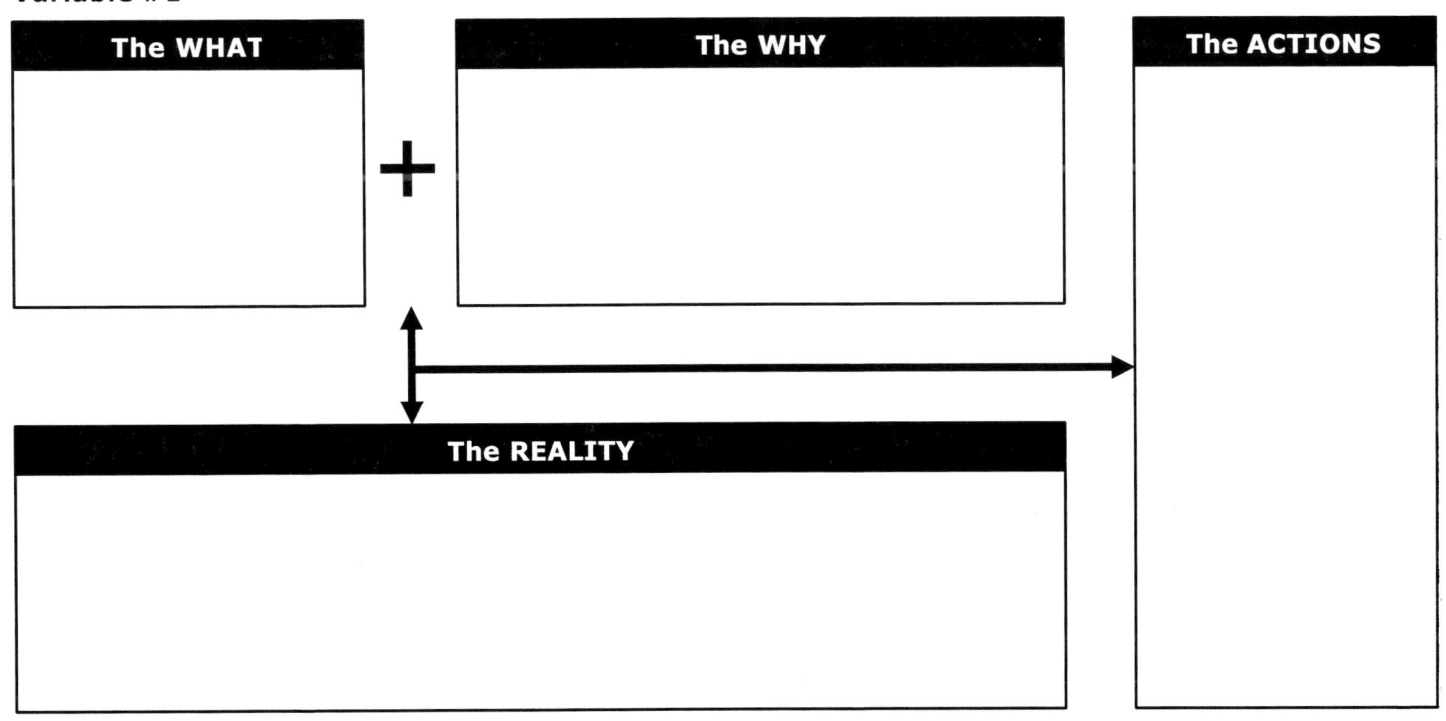

| The WHAT | + | The WHY | | The ACTIONS |

The REALITY

Variable #2

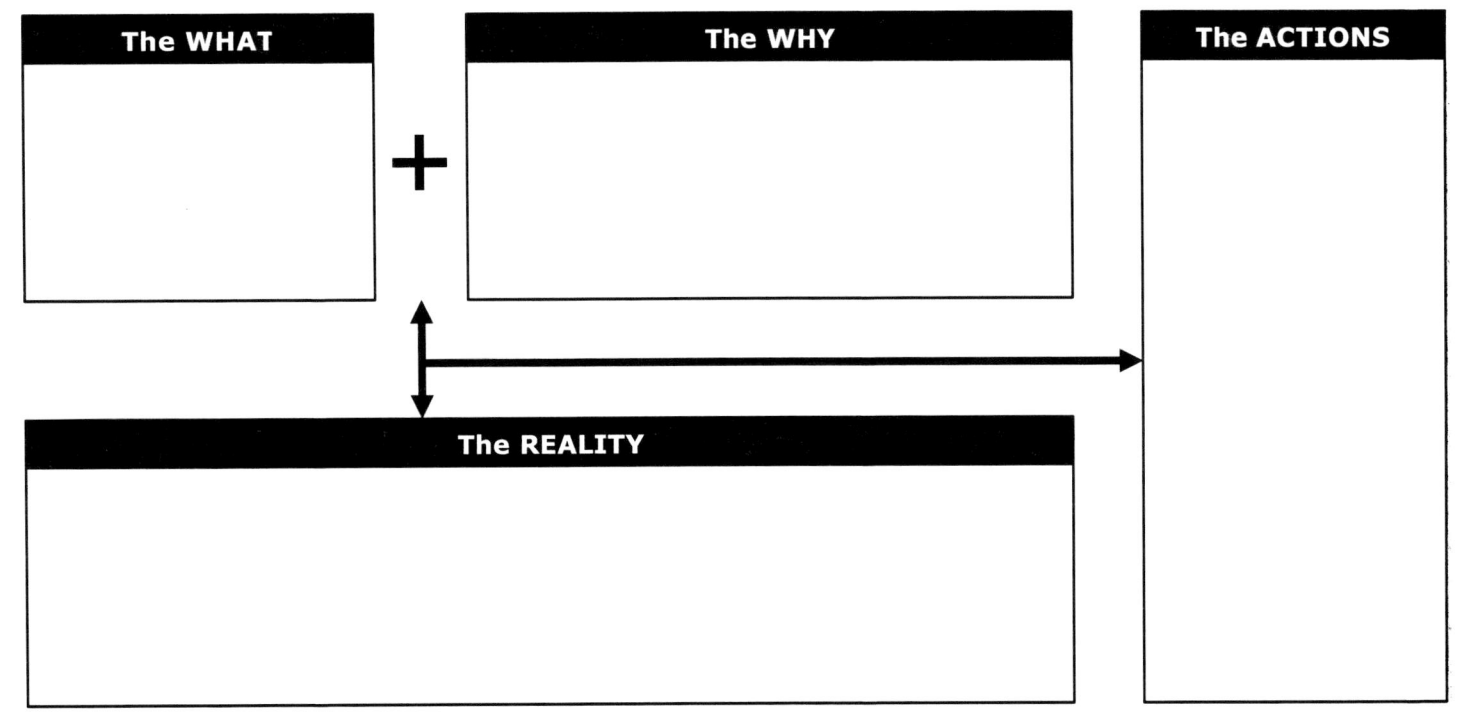

| The WHAT | + | The WHY | | The ACTIONS |

The REALITY

Center for Talent Retention © 2000-2005

Communication

6.13
Communication Cards
Cut out the cards below.

Pay attention to the communication you receive from your manager. When you "experience" one of the actions below, return the card to your manager.

---

(1)

I feel comfortable asking my manager questions and discussing important issues.

(2)

My manager actively listens to me and seeks to understand my point of view.

(3)

My manager often asks for my ideas.

(4)

My manager gets the facts before making judgments or taking action.

Communication

6.13
Communication Action Chart

When you receive the Communication Cards from your team members, check-off the card in the team member's column and record the date you received the card.

As you begin to receive the cards back from your team members think about the following:
- Is there one communication action you do more of or less of?
- Are you more effective at communicating with some team members versus others?
- Who do you need to improve your communication actions with?

Feedback Card	Team Member Name	Team Member Name	Team Member Name	Team Member Name	Team Member Name
(1) I feel comfortable asking my manager questions and discussing important issues	☐ Date received	☐ Date received	☐ Date received	☐ Date received	☐ Date received
(2) My manager actively listens to me and seeks to understand my point of view	☐ Date received	☐ Date received	☐ Date received	☐ Date received	☐ Date received
(3) My manager often asks for my ideas	☐ Date received	☐ Date received	☐ Date received	☐ Date received	☐ Date received
(4) My manager gets the facts before making judgments or taking action	☐ Date received	☐ Date received	☐ Date received	☐ Date received	☐ Date received

Communication

6.14
Mini-Assessment
A little over a month ago I began improving my "communication" capabilities. Please help me gauge my performance by taking 5 minutes to answer a few questions. Please return the assessment with the enclosed envelope.

Thank you for your feedback!

Communication Mini-Assessment
Please evaluate my improvement in the area of "communication".
For each of the following statements, circle the level of change you have noticed in my actions <u>in the last 45 Days</u>.

Am I MORE or LESS effective on the following...

Less Effective		No Perceivable Change		More Effective	Not Applicable
-2	-1	0	+1	+2	NA

I actively listen to you and try to understand your point of view

-2   -1   0   +1   +2   NA

You are comfortable asking me questions and discussing important issues

-2   -1   0   +1   +2   NA

I often ask for your ideas

-2   -1   0   +1   +2   NA

I get the facts before making judgments or taking action

-2   -1   0   +1   +2   NA

I consistently share critical information with the team

-2   -1   0   +1   +2   NA

What else can I do to improve my communication skills?

_____

_____

_____

_____

Communication

6.15
Bust-up the Roadblocks

Record your current and planned communication actions below. Review each action and determine if a "roadblock" or obstacle is preventing you from implementing a planned action or preventing a current action from creating its desired impact. Based on the "roadblock", identify "bust-up" actions you can take to eliminate or manage the roadblock.

Current and Planned Communication Actions	"Roadblock" or Obstacle	"Bust-up" Action

Personal Actions

Manage the way you handle difficult and frustrating situations

Personal Actions

48 Hours

7.1 Talk-it-Up!
Tell your manager, team, and peers you plan to improve your "personal actions"

7.2 Benefit Analysis
Determine whether improving your "personal actions" will be valuable for yourself and others

7.3 Personal Actions Self-Assessment
Identify the actions you need to do "more of" and "less of" to improve your "personal actions"

7.4 Buffer Zone
Identify buffering techniques to use during difficult situations

7 Days

7.5 Two 4 U: Ideas for Improvement
Ask others for two ideas to improve your "personal actions"

7.6 Tracking Chart
Create a tracking chart to capture your "personal actions" progress

7.7 Assess My Personal Actions
Receive input on your personal actions

7.8 Personal Network
Identify a network of people you can turn to during difficult situations

7.9 Lessons Learned
Evaluate past situations in which you struggled to handle a frustrating event

30 Days

7.10 Team Discussion
Facilitate a team discussion to improve your "personal actions"

7.11 Feedback for Me
Receive feedback on your "personal actions"

7.12 Team Feedback
Ask your team to answer "personal actions" questions and present their responses back to you

7.13 Act After 3
Take action to avoid taking frustrations out on others

90 Days

7.14 Mini-Assessment
Assess your "personal actions" progress

7.15 Bust-up the Roadblocks
Identify the obstacles and hurdles preventing you from improving your "personal action"

7.16 Personal Mentor
Use a mentor to help you improve your "personal actions"

7.17 Red Zone
Chart your weekly reactions during your interactions with others

Personal Actions
48 Hours

Prep Time **5 minutes**   *Action Time* **15 minutes**

7.1
Talk-it-Up!
Tell your manager, team, and peers you plan to improve your personal actions

Identify the individuals and/or groups who will be most impacted by a change in your personal actions and share your desire to improve your capabilities.

Step 1: In a team meeting, share your desire to improve your personal actions . Be sure to discuss the following:
- Explain "why" you have chosen to improve your personal actions
- Describe how an increase in performance will help you, the organization, and others
- Outline what you actions you plan to take to impact your capabilities

Step 2: Solicit the groups' help and feedback. Ask them to support your development by focusing on your personal actions from this point forward (not what you did in the past). Ask them to give you feedback on what you are doing well and what you need to improve.

Note: *Talk-it-Up!* is best done face-to-face, however, you can also *Talk-it-Up!* during a conference call or via email.

Personal Actions
48 Hours

Prep Time 5 minutes   *Action Time* 10 minutes

Download electronic copy:
www.keeppeople.com/book/7.2.dot

7.2
Benefit Analysis
Determine whether improving your personal actions will be valuable for yourself and others

Complete a *Benefit Analysis* to determine whether improving your personal actions will be valuable for yourself and others.

Step 1: Identify the key individuals and/or groups who will be most impacted by a change in your personal actions. Record their names on the **Benefit Analysis Square** (page 245).

Step 2: For each individual or group, answer the following question:

> *"If you improve your personal actions, what benefits will be experienced by the individual or group?"*

Identify two benefits for each individual or group, and record your responses on the *Benefit Analysis Square*.

Step 3: After completing the *Benefit Analysis Square*, determine whether the benefits of improving your personal actions outweigh the time and energy needed to improve your performance.

- If YES, move forward and take action to improve your personal actions
- If NO, select another manager capability to improve

Example

Your Employees
1. My employees will not be leery of me during difficult and stressful situations.
2. My employees will feel comfortable sharing "bad news" with me.

Personal Actions
48 Hours

Prep Time 5 minutes **Action Time** 15 minutes

Download electronic copy:
www.keeppeople.com/book/7.3.dot

7.3
Personal Actions Self-Assessment
Identify the actions you need to do "more of" and "less of" to improve your "personal actions"

Determine the actions you must continue and discontinue to improve your "personal actions".

Step 1: Review the situations on the **Personal Actions Self-Assessment** worksheet (page 246), and think about your personal actions and behaviors.

Step 2: For each situation, determine how you currently react to the situation. Think about what really happens most of the time, not what you would like to have happen, or what happens some of the time. If we were a "fly on-the-wall" what would we see? Record your responses on the worksheet.

Step 3: Now think about how you could handle the situations in the future to improve your reactions. Record these actions on the worksheet.

Step 4: Periodically review your self-assessment to determine if you were able to increase the actions you need to do "more of", and reduce or eliminate the actions you need to do "less of".

Note: *We judge ourselves mostly by our intentions—however, others judge us mostly by our actions.*

Example

Personal Action Situations	CURRENT REACTION How I currently act	FUTURE REACTION A better way to handle the situation
When I'm under stress	• I don't take the time to listen to others • I shorten other people's deadlines • I often yell at my employees	• Reduce my daily tasks • Spend 3-5 minutes clearly identifying what I want to say to an employee before I approach him or her

Personal Actions
48 Hours

Prep Time
5 minutes

Action Time
20 minutes

Download electronic copy:
www.keeppeople.com/book/7.4.dot

7.4
Buffer Zone
Identify buffering techniques to use during difficult situations

Identify buffering techniques to use when you're frustrated, angry, or "emotionally charged" from work situations.

Step 1: Identify your person triggers...what work events or situations lead to frustration, anger or high levels of emotions. Record your triggers on the **Buffer Zone** worksheet (page 247).

Step 2: For each trigger, determine what you can do to create a buffer between the trigger and when you respond to it. Record the buffer next to the trigger on the *Buffer Zone* worksheet.

Note: The *Buffer Zone* creates time for you to respond with the right level of emotion <u>and</u> address the situation appropriately and professionally. When a trigger occurs, implement your buffer <u>before</u> you respond to the event or situation.

Example

TRIGGER	BUFFER
An employee treats a customer poorly.	Before talking with the employee, spend 5 minutes to determine what I want to say. Only when I feel calm will I talk with the employee.

Personal Actions
7 Days

Prep Time **5 minutes** *Action Time* **60 minutes**

Download electronic copy:
www.keeppeople.com/book/7.5.dot

7.5
Two 4 U: Ideas for Improvement
Ask others for two ideas to improve your personal actions

Using the wisdom and experience from others, generate as many ideas as possible to improve your personal actions.

Step 1: Identify up to 5 people who have excellent personal actions.

Step 2: Ask each person the following question:

"I'm trying to improve my personal actions, do you have two ideas for how I can improve my capabilities?"

Step 3: Record each person's ideas on the **Two 4 U** worksheet (page 248).

Step 4: Once you gathered ideas from each person, review the suggestions and circle the top three ideas you think will help the most.

Step 5: For your top three ideas, identify the next steps you will take to implement the idea.

Step 6: Thank the individuals who gave you the development ideas and share what actions you plan to take to improve your personal actions.

Personal Actions
7 Days

Prep Time **5 minutes**   *Action Time* **10 minutes**

Download electronic copy:
www.keeppeople.com/book/7.6.dot

7.6
Tracking Chart
Create a tracking chart to capture your personal actions progress

Each Friday capture what you actually completed during the week to improve your personal actions.

Step 1: Each Friday, identify and record the actions you took to improve your performance on the **Tracking Chart** (page 249).

Step 2: For each action, grade your performance based on how well you think you performed on the action, as well as considering feedback you may have received from others.

A = Excellent; B = Good; C = Average; D = Poor; F = Failing

Step 3: Based on your performance, identify one improvement action you will implement the following week.

Step 4: After completing the *Tracking Chat* ask yourself the following questions:
- Am I really taking actions to improve?
- Are my actions having the desired impact on my personal actions?

Example

Week	Personal Actions	Grade
December 11	Used my buffer technique before responding to accusations from my manager	B
	Asked an employee for two ideas for how I can improve my personal actions	A
	Expressed inappropriate anger when Karen told me she would miss an important deadline	F
Improvement Actions • Talk with Karen about my earlier "blow-up"		

Personal Actions
7 Days

Prep Time
5 minutes

Action Time
60 minutes

7.7
Assess My Personal Actions
Receive input on your personal actions

Ask your team members to evaluate your personal actions.

Step 1: Send the following email to your team members:

I am currently working to improve my "personal actions", and would like your help. Please take five minutes to evaluate my personal actions by answering the following questions:

1. *On a scale of 1 to 10 (1=Red Hot; 10=Cool, Calm, and Collected)*
   - *How would you rate my ability to handle personal frustrations?*
2. *What ideas do you have for me to improve my ability to handle frustrating situations?*

Step 2: Follow-up with each team member (face-to-face or phone call) to discuss your personal actions with the team member. During the follow-up discussion, identify actions you will take to improve your personal actions with each team member.

Personal Actions
7 Days

Prep Time
5 minutes

Action Time
20 minutes

Download electronic copy:
www.keeppeople.com/book/7.8.dot

7.8
Personal Network
Identify a network of people you can turn to during difficult situations

Create a *Personal Network* of individuals who you can turn to when you need help with a difficult or stressful situation.

Step 1: Using the **Personal Network** worksheet (page 250), think of two people who are great at handle difficult and frustrating situations <u>and</u> could provide you help when you are faced with a difficult situation.

Step 2: For each person, determine what specific issues they can help you with and record their name and the issues on the worksheet.

Note: Use your *Personal Network* as needed to help diffuse situations, provide feedback on past events, and brainstorm actions you can take to improve your ability to handle stressful and difficult situations.

Personal Actions
7 Days

Prep Time
5 minutes

Action Time
25 minutes

Download electronic copy:
www.keeppeople.com/book/7.9.dot

7.9
Lessons Learned
Evaluate past situations in which you struggled to handle a frustrating event

Learn how to improve your "personal actions" by identifying three situations in which you struggled to handle a frustrating or stress event.

Step 1: Think about your previous work situations. Identify three situations that were stressful, frustrating, and or created irritation. Record the events on the **Lessons Learned** worksheet (page 251).

Step 2: For each event, identify and record the actions you took to handle the situation.

Step 3: Identify the impact your actions created for yourself and others.

Step 4: Outline what you could have done differently to handle the situation better.

Step 5: Determine what outcome would have occurred if the "new actions" you identified had been implemented in the situation.

Step 6: Based on your *Lessons Learned*, identify the actions you want to implement to ensure you improve your ability to handle stressful and difficult situations.

Example

EVENT	My Actions	Impact on Self and Others	What could have be done differently	Potential Outcome
My director shortened the deadline for Project Z	I immediately started yelling at my team to make Project Z a priority. I told an employee he was working too slowly.	Employees feel frustrated, angry, unappreciated, and stressed. I am stressed and not in control of my emotions and behaviors.	Identify what needs to happen to meet the deadline. Ask my team for help—ask them what we have to do to meet the deadline.	I will not react irrationally. The team will help identify the solution. I will be less stressed and in control.

236

Center for Talent Retention © 2001-2005

Personal Actions
30 Days

Prep Time
5 minutes

Action Time
45 minutes

7.10
Team Discussion
Facilitate a team discussion to improve your personal actions

Solicit ideas from your team to improve your personal actions, and identify a way to receive immediate feedback as you implement your personal actions.

Step 1: In a team meeting share "why" you want to improve your personal actions, and share your thoughts about the importance of personal actions.

Step 2: Ask your team members to share how they think your personal actions impact the team and individual team members.

Step 3: Ask the team to brainstorm actions you can take to improve your personal actions.

Step 4: With the team, identify a way for team members to cue you when your actions are consistent, as well as inconsistent with the desired personal actions.

Try pick two hand gestures, statements, or signals to indicate when the new personal actions are happening and when they're not.

For example, team members may say *"Right on!"* when your behaviors are consistent, and *"Take a step back"* when your behaviors are inconsistent. Teams members may also use a hand gesture such as "thumbs-up" or "thumbs-down".

Personal Actions
30 Days

Prep Time **5 minutes** *Action Time* **2 hours**

Download electronic copy:
www.keeppeople.com/book/7.11.dot

7.11
Feedback for Me
Receive feedback on your personal actions

Solicit feedback on the actions you have taken to improve your personal actions.

Step 1: Identify up to 5 people who can give you feedback on your personal actions, and send them the following email:

> *I have chosen to take action to improve my personal actions and would like some help from you. In the next 30 to 45 days, I'd like to follow-up with you to receive feedback on my "personal action" performance. When we talk, I will ask you the following questions:*
> 1. *What personal actions have you seen me perform?*
> 2. *What impact have my actions created for individuals, the team, and/or the organization?*
> 3. *What improvement ideas do you have for me?*
>
> *Thank you for your help. I look forward to speaking with you soon.*

Step 2: Identify a follow-up date when you will ask each person for feedback. Record the date on the **Feedback for Me** worksheet (page 252).

Step 3: At the time of your follow-up dates, schedule a 15 minute discussion with each person to receive feedback on your personal actions.

Step 4: After receiving feedback, record the feedback on the *Feedback for Me* worksheet. Be sure to thank each person for his or her time and willingness to provide you feedback on your personal actions.

Step 5: Based on the feedback you received, think about the following:
- What personal actions do I need to do more of?
- What actions do I need to do less of?
- What additional actions should I integrate into my personal actions improvement plan?

Personal Actions
30 Days

Prep Time
10 minutes

Action Time
90 minutes

Download electronic copy:
www.keeppeople.com/book/7.12.dot

7.12
Team Feedback
Ask your team to answer "personal actions" questions and present their responses back to you

Facilitate a feedback session with your team to understand how your "personal actions" impact others.

Step 1: In a team meeting, explain why you have chosen to improve your "personal actions" and share your thoughts regarding the importance of "personal actions".

Step 2: Ask your team to discuss and summarize the statements on the **Team Feedback** worksheet (page 253).

Step 3: LEAVE THE ROOM. Your team should discuss the questions without you. This process will provide the most honest feedback to help you improve your "personal actions".

Step 4: After you leave the room, each team member should spend 10 minutes thinking about his or her own responses to the *Team Feedback* questions.

Step 5: The group should then summarize the individual responses; adding, deleting, or modifying responses to create a concise group summary.

Step 6: After summarizing the responses, the group should invite you back into the room to review their *Team Feedback* summary.

Step 7: Based on the team discussion, identify and share the actions you will take in the future to improve your "personal actions". Thank the team for their honest feedback.

Personal Actions
30 Days

Prep Time
1 minute

Action Time
1 minute

Download electronic copy:
www.keeppeople.com/book/7.13.dot

7.13
Act After 3
Take action to avoid taking frustrations out on others

When frustrating events occur, take 60 to 90 seconds to ensure you avoid taking frustrations out on others..

Step 1: When a frustrating or difficult situation occurs, jot down one or two words to describe the situation on the **Act After 3** worksheet (page 254).

Step 2: Outline possible actions you can take to address the situation.

Step 3: Identify the best action you can take and determine how you will implement the solution.

Note:
- Taking 60 to 90 seconds to complete these three steps will help you take the best action versus reacting inappropriately.
- You may want to have copies of the *Act After 3* worksheet handy to enable you to can complete the exercise in under 2 minutes.

Example

STEP 1 The Situation	STEP 2 Action Options	STEP 3 Best Action
Chris "dropped the ball"	• Yell at Chris • Do it myself • Talk to Chris	Schedule time this afternoon to talk with Chris

Personal Actions
90 Days

Prep Time **10 minutes** *Action Time* **30 minutes**

Download electronic copy:
www.keeppeople.com/book/7.14.pdf

7.14
Mini-Assessment
Assess your personal actions performance progress

Determine if your personal actions are perceived as more effective.

45 Days Before the Mini-Assessment:
Step 1: Identify the individuals and/or groups who will be most impacted by a change in your personal actions and share your desire to improve your personal actions.

Step 2: Explain "why" you have chosen to improve your personal actions. Describe how an increase in performance will help you, the organization, and others.

Step 3: Solicit their help and feedback. Ask the individuals to support your development by observing your actions for 45 days. Tell them at the end of the 45 days you will give them a *Mini-Assessment* to evaluate your personal actions.

The Mini-Assessment:
Step 4: After 45 days, give a copy of the **Mini-Assessment** (page 255) to the individuals you asked to observe your behaviors—ask them to complete the *Mini-Assessment* honestly.

Step 5: Request the individuals return the assessment to you when they are finished.

Step 6: Summarize your results for each statement. Where do you have strengths and weaknesses?

Step 7: Identify actions you will take based on your *Mini-Assessment* results.

Step 8: Share these actions with the individuals who gave you feedback and thank them for their help.

Personal Actions
90 Days

Prep Time **5 minutes** *Action Time* **10 minutes**

Download electronic copy:
www.keeppeople.com/book/7.15.dot

7.15
Bust-up the Roadblocks
Identify the obstacles and hurdles preventing you from improving your personal actions

Identify why you may not be taking action to improve your personal actions, and/or determine why the actions you have taken are not having the desired impact.

Step 1: Record your current and planned personal actions on the **Bust-up the Roadblocks** worksheet (page 256).

Step 2: Review each action and determine if a "roadblock" or obstacle is preventing you from implementing a planned action or preventing a current action from creating its desired impact.

Step 3: Based on the "roadblock", identify "bust-up" actions you can take to eliminate or manage the roadblock.

Example

Current and Planned Personal Action	"Roadblock" or Obstacle	"Bust-up" Action
I plan to tap into my Personal Network	My schedule is so crazy during the day, I have not made the time to meet with the people in my Personal Network	I will send an email to the individuals in my Personal Network to get some time scheduled on my calendar for us to meet.

Personal Actions
90 Days

Prep Time **10 minutes**

Action Time **TBD**

7.16
Personal Mentor
Use a mentor to help you improve your "personal actions"

Identify a person who has great "personal actions" and is willing to help you build your capabilities

Step 1: Identify a person who you are currently working with or have worked with in the past who has excellent "personal actions".

Step 2: Ask the individual if he or she would be willing to help you over the next 60 days to improve your "personal actions".

Step 3: As difficult or frustrating situations occur, implement at least one of the following actions:

1. **Before** you take action, plan how you will react to the situation and present your plan to your mentor. Ask for additional methods or ideas for handling the situation.

2. **After** reacting to the situation, share the experience with your mentor. Identify the strengths and weaknesses of your actions, and outline future actions that would improve future situations.

Note: Working with a mentor will help you identify the areas you need to improve, while gaining valuable insight and wisdom from an expert.

Personal Actions
90 Days

Prep Time
5 minutes

Action Time
20 minutes

Download electronic copy:
www.keeppeople.com/book/7.17.pdf

7.17
Red Zone
Chart your weekly reactions during your interactions with others

Chart your reactions with others in meetings, during phones, and in face-to-face Interactions, to determine how well you are handling difficult and stressful situations.

Step 1: Each week, think about the meetings, people interactions, and phone calls you had during the week. For each interaction, determine the following:
- Your level of feelings during the event
- Your level of actions in response to the event

Step 2: Using the **Red Zone** worksheet (page 257), chart each interaction based on your level of feelings and actions; placing the interaction in the appropriate quadrant.

Step 3: Once your interactions are mapped on the chart, think about the following:
1. What quadrant are most of your interactions?
2. What events fall in the RED ZONE? Is there a connection between the situations?
3. What situations are easy for you to handle?
4. Do certain events (e.g., face-to-face meetings or budget discussions) trigger more emotion?

Step 4: Based on your *Red Zone* review, determine what actions you can take in the following week to reduce your number of RED ZONE events.

Personal Actions

7.2
Benefit Analysis Square

For each individual or group, answer the following question:

"If you improve personal actions,, what benefits will be experienced by the individual or group?"

Identify two benefits for each individual or group, and record your responses below.

Determine whether the benefits of improving your "personal actions" outweigh the time and energy needed to improve your performance.

- If YES, move forward and take action to improve your "personal actions"
- If NO, select another manager capability to improve

Yourself	Your Manager	Your Employees
1.	1.	1.
2.	2.	2.

Your Peers & Co-Workers		Key Customers & Clients
1.	**Benefits**	1.
2.		2.

Your Significant Other/Family	Other _____	Other _____
1.	1.	1.
2.	2.	2.

Personal Actions

7.3
Personal Actions Self-Assessment

Review the situations below, and think about your personal actions and behaviors. For each situation, determine how you currently react to the situation. Think about what really happens most of the time, not what you would like to have happen, or what happens some of the time. If we were a "fly on-the-wall" what would we see? Record your responses on the worksheet.

Now think about how you could handle the situations in the future to improve your reactions. Record these actions on the worksheet.

Personal Action Situations	CURRENT REACTION *How I currently act*	FUTURE REACTION *A better way to handle the situation*
When I'm under stress		
When I receive critical feedback		
When I miss a deadline		
When someone disagrees with me		
When I'm behind schedule or late		
When other people overreact		

Personal Actions

7.4
Buffer Zone

Identify your person triggers...what work events or situations lead to frustration, anger or high levels of emotions. Record your triggers below. For each trigger, determine what you can do to create a buffer between the trigger and when you respond to it. Record the buffer next to the trigger below.

TRIGGER	BUFFER

Personal Actions

7.5
Two 4 U

Identify up to 5 people who have excellent "personal action" and ask each person the following question:

"I'm trying to improve my "personal actions", do you have two ideas for how I can improve my personal actions?"

Record each person's ideas below. Once you gathered ideas from each person, review the suggestions and circle the top three ideas you think will help the most.

For your top three ideas, identify the next steps you will take to implement the idea.

Individual	Idea #1	Idea #2	Next Steps

Personal Actions

7.6
Tracking Chart

Each Friday, identify and record the actions you took to improve your performance. For each action, grade your performance based on how well you think you performed on the action, as well as considering feedback you may have received from others.

A = Excellent; B = Good; C = Average; D = Poor; F = Failing

Based on your performance, identify one improvement action you will implement the following week.

Week	Personal Actions	Grade

Improvement Action:

Week	Personal Actions	Grade

Improvement Action:

Week	Personal Actions	Grade

Improvement Action:

Personal Actions

7.8
Personal Network
Think of two people who are great at handle difficult and frustrating situations <u>and</u> could provide you help when you are faced with a difficult situation. For each person, determine what specific issues they can help you with and record their name and the issues below.

	Personal Actions Resource #1
Name	
Situation or Issue	
	Personal Actions Resource #2
Name	
Situation or Issue	

Personal Actions

7.9
Lessons Learned

Think about your previous work situations. Identify three situations that were stressful, frustrating, and or created irritation. Record the events below. For each event, identify and record the actions you took to handle the situation. Identify the impact your actions created for yourself and others. Outline what you could have done differently to handle the situation better. Determine what outcome would have occurred if the "new actions" you identified had been implemented in the situation.

EVENT	My Actions	Impact on Self and Others	What could have be done differently	Potential Outcome

Personal Actions

7.10
Feedback for Me

Identify up to 5 people who can give you feedback on your "personal actions". Determine when you will follow-up with each person and record the date below.

After receiving feedback, record the feedback from each person.

Based on the feedback you received, think about the following:
- What "personal actions" do I need to do more of?
- What actions do I need to do less of?
- What additional actions should I integrate into my "personal actions" improvement plan?

Name	Follow-Up Date	Feedback		
		What "personal actions" have you seen me perform?	What impact have my actions created for individuals, the team, and/or the organization?	What improvement ideas do you have for me?

Personal Actions

7.12
Team Feedback

Review the following "personal actions" statements. Based on your manager's actions, jot down your responses to each question. Share your responses with the team to create an overall team response for each question.

"Personal Actions" Statements	Response
You handle yourself POORLY when _____ happens…	
You handle yourself WELL when _____ happens…	
You are "out of control" when _____ happens…	
You need to get better at handling _____ situations…	
You are calm, cool, and collected when…	

Personal Actions

7.13
Act After 3

When a frustrating or difficult situation occurs, jot down one or two words to describe the situation on below. Outline possible actions you can take to address the situation. Identify the best action you can take and determine how you will implement the solution.

STEP 1 The Situation	STEP 2 Action Options	STEP 3 Best Action

Personal Action

7.14
Mini-Assessment

A little over a month ago I began improving my "personal actions". Please help me gauge my performance by taking 5 minutes to answer a few questions. Please return the assessment with the enclosed envelope.

Thank you for your feedback!

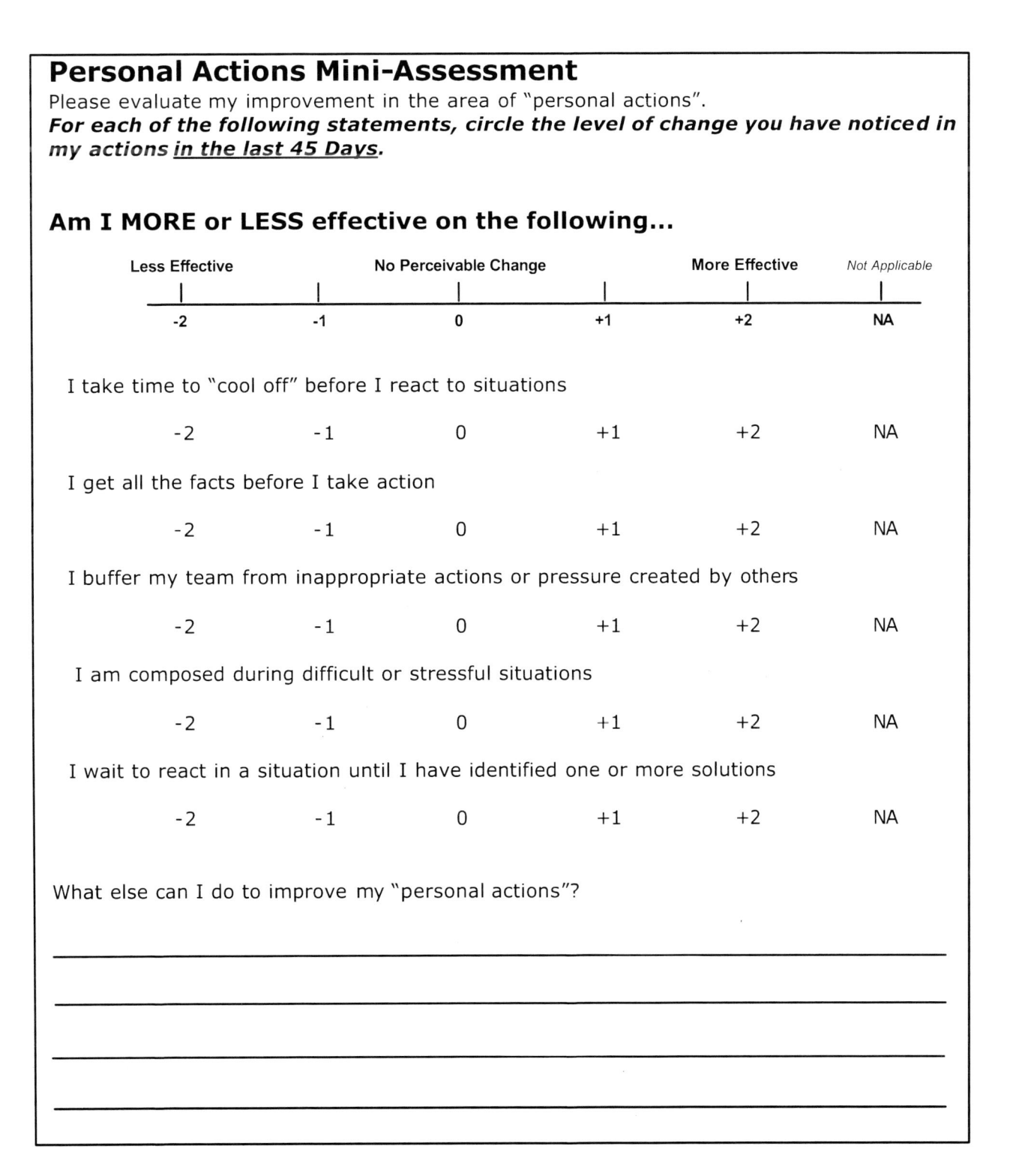

Personal Actions Mini-Assessment

Please evaluate my improvement in the area of "personal actions".
For each of the following statements, circle the level of change you have noticed in my actions <u>in the last 45 Days</u>.

Am I MORE or LESS effective on the following...

Less Effective		No Perceivable Change		More Effective	Not Applicable
-2	-1	0	+1	+2	NA

I take time to "cool off" before I react to situations

    -2   -1   0   +1   +2   NA

I get all the facts before I take action

    -2   -1   0   +1   +2   NA

I buffer my team from inappropriate actions or pressure created by others

    -2   -1   0   +1   +2   NA

I am composed during difficult or stressful situations

    -2   -1   0   +1   +2   NA

I wait to react in a situation until I have identified one or more solutions

    -2   -1   0   +1   +2   NA

What else can I do to improve my "personal actions"?

_____

_____

_____

_____

Personal Actions

7.15
Bust-up the Roadblocks

Record your current and planned "personal actions" below. Review each action and determine if a "roadblock" or obstacle is preventing you from implementing a planned action or preventing a current action from creating its desired impact. Based on the "roadblock", identify "bust-up" actions you can take to eliminate or manage the roadblock.

Current and Planned Personal Actions	"Roadblock" or Obstacle	"Bust-up" Action

Personal Actions

7.17
Red Zone

Each week, think about the meetings, people interactions, and phone calls you had during the week. For each interaction, determine the following:
- Your level of feelings during the event
- Your level of actions in response to the event

Chart each interaction based on your level of feelings and actions; placing the interaction in the appropriate quadrant below.

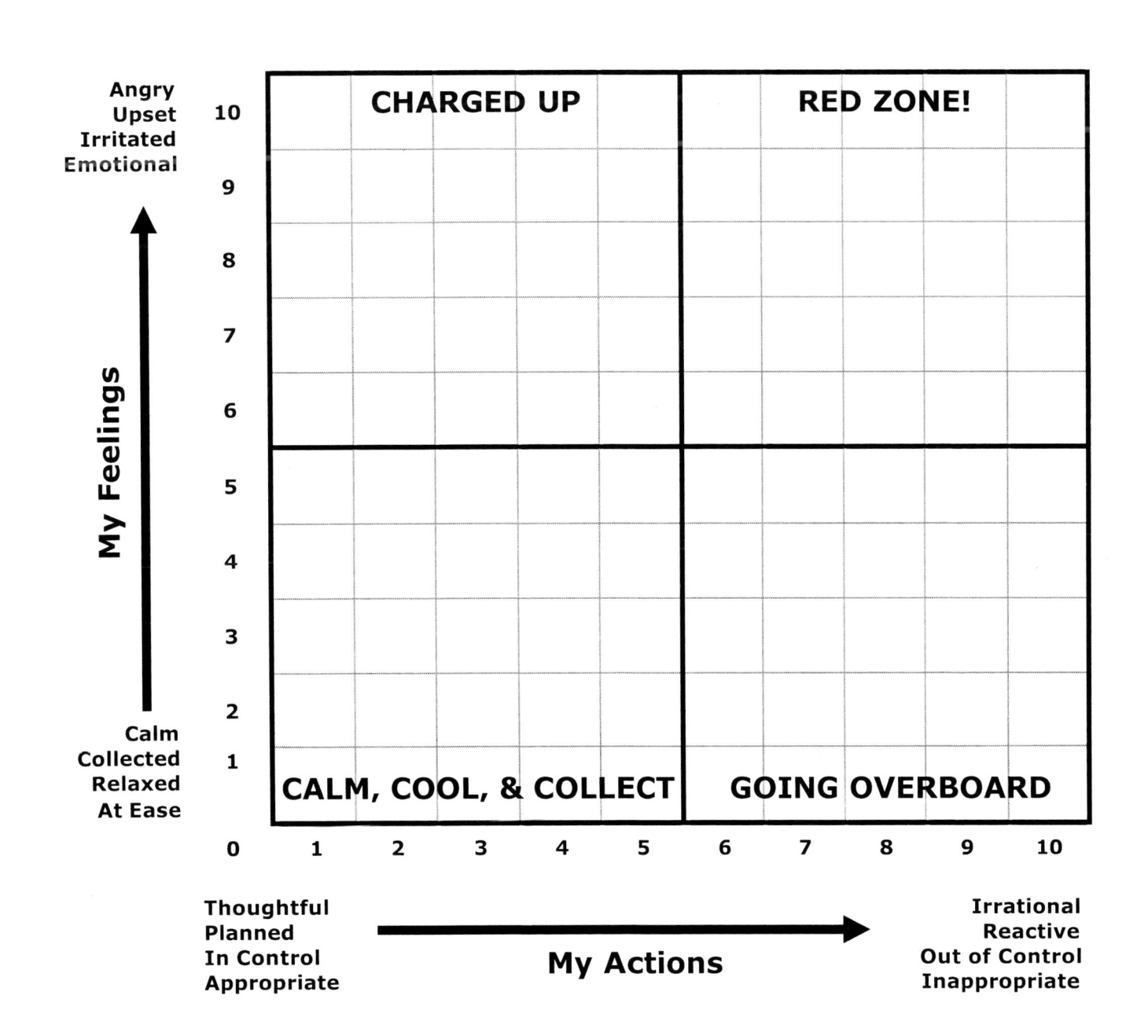

My Feelings (y-axis, 0–10):
- Top (10): Angry, Upset, Irritated, Emotional
- Bottom (1): Calm, Collected, Relaxed, At Ease

My Actions (x-axis, 0–10):
- Left: Thoughtful, Planned, In Control, Appropriate
- Right: Irrational, Reactive, Out of Control, Inappropriate

Quadrants:
- Top-left: **CHARGED UP**
- Top-right: **RED ZONE!**
- Bottom-left: **CALM, COOL, & COLLECT**
- Bottom-right: **GOING OVERBOARD**

Center for Talent Retention © 2000-2005